Dolphins & Porpoises

Dolphins & Porpoises

A WORLDWIDE GUIDE

Jean-Pierre Sylvestre

Sterling Publishing Co., Inc. New York

Front cover photo by F. Gohier

overleaf: graceful in flight, the orca (orcinus orca) *in a bay on the west coast of Canada*
facing page: A couple of large dolphins
(Tursiops truncatus)

Library of Congress Cataloging-in-Publication Data

Sylvestre, Jean-Pierre.
  [Guide des dauphins et marsouins. English]
  Dolphins & porpoises : a worldwide guide / Jean-Pierre Sylvestre ;
[translated by Catherine Berthier].
        p.   cm.
  Includes bibliographical references (p.   ) and index.
  ISBN 0-8069-8791-X
  1. Dolphins. 2. Porpoises. 3. River dolphins.   I. Title.
II. Title: Dolphins and porpoises.
QL737.C432S9313   1993
599.5′3—dc20   93-24789
                                                                CIP

Translated by Catherine Berthier

10 9 8 7 6 5 4 3 2

Published 1993 by Sterling Publishing Company, Inc.
387 Park Avenue South, New York, N.Y. 10016
Originally published in Switzerland by Delachaux & Niestlé S.A.
under the title *Guide des dauphins et marsouins*
© 1990 by Delachaux & Niestlé, David Perret, editor
Neuchâtel (Switzerland)-Paris
English translation and additional photographs
© 1993 by Sterling Publishing Company, Inc.
Distributed in Canada by Sterling Publishing
% Canadian Manda Group, P.O. Box 920, Station U
Toronto, Ontario, Canada M8Z 5P9
Distributed in Great Britain and Europe by Cassell PLC
Villiers House, 41/47 Strand, London WC2N 5JE, England
Distributed in Australia by Capricorn Link Ltd.
P.O. Box 665, Lane Cove, NSW 2066
Printed and bound in Hong Kong
All rights reserved

Sterling ISBN 0-8069-8791-X

CONTENTS

INTRODUCTION

This volume deals with the dolphins and porpoises that inhabit our seas and oceans and even some of our rivers. If whales have impressed the popular imagination with their size, dolphins have always excited curiosity and sympathy. Whether it is due to television, books, or movies, this cetacean enjoys an exceptional popularity with the Western public.

The dolphin has always been revered, as is demonstrated by its presence in art through antiquity. But the question of how well we know this marine mammal, which many mistakenly call "fish," remains. For example, how many people know that there are in fact more than 30 dolphin species? Our knowledge of cetology is still deficient, and it is vital that scientists continue with their research.

Dolphins are fashionable and seen everywhere, but this type of fad has its negative aspects. The information offered by the press and nonspecialized media is often studded with inaccuracies, giving the public ideas that are often far removed from reality.

This book does not pretend to be an exhaustive treatise; it is, rather, an attempt to bring together most of the scientific knowledge available on each species and to make it accessible to the greater public, so that people will have a precise idea of the reality of these extraordinary animals.

There are references to discoveries of Chinese origin throughout the book. Those concerning endemic species have not been published until now. It was my good fortune to have spent six weeks in the People's Republic of China in the fall of 1987. Now, with the publication of this book, my thoughts turn back to the colleagues and friends with whom I had such enriching contact, both at the scientific and human levels, be they cetologists, ichthyologists, museum curators, or academics. I am eager to pay tribute to them here, for, without their help, many facts would be absent from this book.

Jean-Pierre Sylvestre
Montreal, Paris
June 1989

HISTORY OF THE DOLPHIN

Man and the Dolphin

Man has always been affected by the dolphin. During antiquity this animal practically invaded civilization through the arts, as its image was represented in painting, sculpture, pottery, mosaics, and even coins. The dolphin is the marine animal most often represented in the decorations of ancient Greece and Crete. It is also the hero of numerous legends, fables, and myths. Some have described the dolphin as a savior (Odysseus's son Telemachus, the poet Arion), while others have portrayed it as a friend (Dionysus was surrounded by dolphins, and Neptune used the help of one to seduce and marry Amphitrite). In every civilization, we find stories of a man reincarnated as a dolphin, and, to this day, tales of shipwrecks and drowning accidents avoided thanks to dolphins abound.

The dolphin has also left its mark on history. Some European cities have included images of dolphins in their coats of arms. In France, the king's son and heir to the throne was called *Le Dauphin* from the fourteenth century until the Revolution (1789). During the nineteenth century, soldiers in the French marines were nicknamed *marsouins* (porpoises) and used a likeness of the animal as their symbol.

During the course of history, little scientific attention was paid to the dolphin, despite the interest it generated in legends and as food. Most considered it simply as a fish that, along with other cetaceans, could be eaten during Lent and on Fridays. Only Aristotle (384–322 B.C.) and Pliny the Elder (23–79 B.C.) challenged this "classification."

It wasn't until 1551 that a French researcher named Pierre Belon du Mans classified the dolphin as a "fish with lungs." The system of nomenclature for the classification of living things did not yet exist, as the Swedish naturalist Carl von Linnaeus invented it in the eighteenth century. Since then, the blossoming of scientific articles and zoological treatises have allowed dolphins, porpoises, whales, and sperm whales to take their definitive place in the realm of zoological knowledge, especially since the nineteenth century.

Classification

Aquatic mammals, cetaceans include whales, dolphins, porpoises, and related forms that have a large head, a fishlike and almost hairless body, and paddle-shaped forelimbs. Cetaceans are classified into three suborders: the Archeoceti (ancient whales, now extinct), the Mysticeti (baleen whales) and the Odontoceti (toothed whales). The animals described in this book all belong to the Odontoceti suborder. They have no molars and only use their teeth to seize and handle their prey before swallowing it, although the killer whale also uses its teeth to rip its prey's flesh apart. The Odontoceti suborder comprises six families, 33 genera (34 according to some), and more than 60 species.

Classification of these suborders is complex and not completely codified, thus varying from one researcher to the next. Some researchers, the Japanese in particular, have created new families on the basis of anatomical details. This is the case for killer and pilot whales, which they have classified among the Globicephalidae. Other, usually Western, cetologists classify members of the Platanistidae and Phocoenicidae families as Delphinidae. The classification adopted here follows the international model accepted by most ce-

12

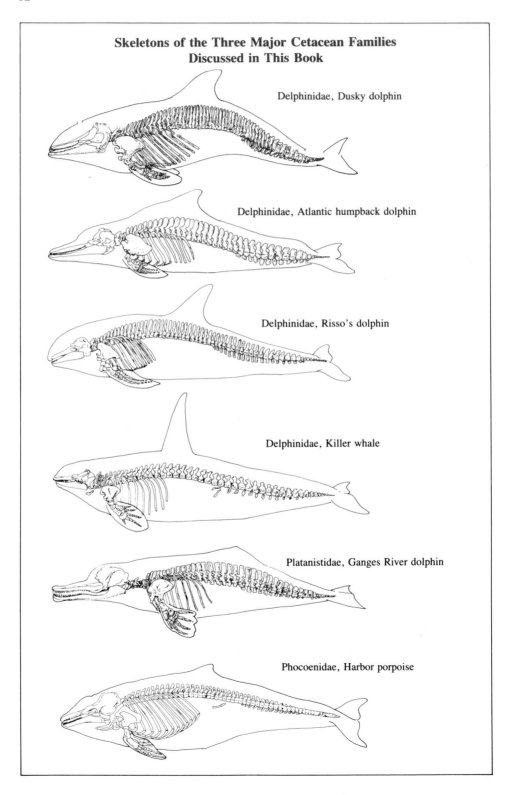

**Skeletons of the Three Major Cetacean Families
Discussed in This Book**

Delphinidae, Dusky dolphin

Delphinidae, Atlantic humpback dolphin

Delphinidae, Risso's dolphin

Delphinidae, Killer whale

Platanistidae, Ganges River dolphin

Phocoenidae, Harbor porpoise

tologists. What follows are its main lines.

The first and least known family is that of the Platanistidae. These are mostly fluvial (river-dwelling) cetaceans found only in Asia and South America. This family comprises five species, which are the oldest living toothed cetaceans. Their snouts are long and thin and measure one-sixth to one-seventh of their total body length. Their cervical vertebrae are articulated, which allows for head mobility, and they have a distinct neck. The eyes in some Platanistidae are shrunken, and the dorsal fin is long and low.

The Delphinidae family comprises the most species within the cetacean order, including dolphins themselves. Many in this family have a beak, or snout, and their size varies from approximately 5 ft. to 26 or 29 ft. (1.5 m to 8 or 9 m). All are carnivorous, feeding on fish (ichtyophagous) and cephalopods, such as squid, cuttle fish, and octopus (teutophagous). In most of these species, only the first two cervical vertebrae are fused.

The third and last family discussed in this book is the Phocoenidae, or porpoises. They are conspicuous by their lack of a snout and by their more than five fused cervical vertebrae. Their jaws are of equal length, and they are smaller than members of the other families, usually under 8 ft. (2.45 m).

Paleontology

We have discovered very few fossilized skeletons from the first cetaceans, and there is little data allowing us to authoritatively link any particular fossil species to a specific present-day species. But it is believed that these marine mammals' ancestors were land-dwelling mammals, probably ungulates, such as primitive mammals of the Mesonychidae family that populated the earth 50 million years ago.

Evolution of the Skull and Blowhole in Cetaceans (from Minasian, 1984)

Mesonychidae (–50 million years), with the sturdy, nonspecialized skull of a carnivorous land-dwelling mammal.

Protocetidae (–50 million years), have adapted to marine life, in particular with the evolution of a "beak," or rostrum.

Dorudontidae (–40 million years), were well-adapted to marine life. The "beak" appears, and the nostrils move back.

Squalodontidae (shark-toothed dolphins, –25 million years), had many of the characteristics of present-day toothed whales, including a blowhole close to the top of the skull.

Modern dolphins appeared 15 million years ago, with the shape of the skull becoming more precise and the teeth more complex.

CLASSIFICATION OF THE CETACEAN ORDER

Suborder: *Mysticeti*, **Baleen whales**
Family: *Balaenidae* (**Right whales**)

- Genus : *Eubalena*
    Species : *E. glacialis*, Right whale
- Genus : *Balaena*
    Species : *B. mysticetus* Bowhead whale
- Genus : *Caperea*
    Species : *C. marginata*, Pygmy right whale

Family: *Eschrichtiidae* (**Grey whales**)

- Genus : *Estrichtius*
    Species : *E. robustus*, Grey whale

Family: *Balaenopteridae* (**Rorqual whales**)

- Genus : *Balaenoptera*
    Species : *B. physalus*, Fin whale
    B. musculus, Blue whale
    B. acurtorostrate, Minke whale
    B. borealis, Sei whale
    B. edeni, Bryde's whale
- Genus : *Megaptera*
    Species : *M. noveangliae*, Humpback whale

Suborder: *Odontoceti*, **Toothed whales**
Family: *Physeteridae* (**Sperm whales**)

- Genus : *Physeter*
    Species : *P. catodon*, Sperm whale
- Genus : *Kogia*
    Species : *K. breviceps*, Pygmy sperm whale
    K. sinus, Dwarf sperm whale

Family: *Ziphiidae* (**Beaked and bottlenosed whales**)

- Genus : *Tasmacetus*
    Species : *T. sheperdi*, Sheperd's beaked whale
- Genus : *Mesoplodon*
    Species : *M. pacificus*, Longman's beaked whale
    M. layardii, Strap-toothed whale
    M. densirostris, Blainville's beaked whale
    M. bowdoini, Andrew's beaked whale

M. stejnegeri, Stejneger's beaked whale
M. grayi, Gray's beaked whale
M. gingkodens, Gingko-toothed beaked whale
M. carlhubbsi, Hubbs's beaked whale
M. europaeus, Gervais's beaked whale
M. miros, True's beaked whale
M. hectori, Hector's beaked whale
M. bidens, Sowerby's beaked whale

- Genus : *Ziphius*
    Species : *Z. cavoristros*, Cuvier's beaked whale
- Genus : *Berardius*
    Species : *B. arnuxii*, Arnoux's beaked whale
    B. bairdii, Baird's beaked whale
- Genus : *Hyperoodon*
    Species : *H. planifrons*, Southern bottlenose whale
    H. ampullatus, Northern bottlenose whale

Family: *Monodontidae*

- Genus : *Monodon*
    Species : *M. monoceros*, Narwal
- Genus : *Delphinapterus*
    Species : *D. leucas*, Beluga

Family: *Platanistidae* (**Freshwater dolphins**)

- Genus : *Platanista*
    Species : *P. gangetica*, Ganges River dolphin
    P. minor, Indus River dolphin
- Genus : *Inia*
    Species : *I. geoffrensis*, Amazon River dolphin
- Genus : *Pontoporia*
    Species : *P. blainvillei*, Plata River dolphin

- Genus : *Lipotes*
  - Species : *L. vexifiller*, Baiji River dolphin

Family: *Delphinidae* (Dolphins)

- Genus : *Orcaella*
  - Species : *O. brevirostris*, Irrawaddy dolphin
- Genus : *Steno*
  - Species : *Steno bredanensis*, Rough-toothed dolphin
- Genus : *Sousa*
  - Species : *S. chinensis*, Indo-Pacific humpback dolphin
    - *S. teuszii*, Atlantic humpback dolphin
- Genus : *Sotalia*
  - Species : *Sotalia fluviatilis*, Tucuxi dolphin
- Genus: : *Lagenorhynchus*
  - Species : *L. australis*, Peale's dolphin
    - *L. cruciger*, Hourglass dolphin
    - *L. obscurus*, Dusky dolphin
    - *L. obliquidens*, Pacific white-sided dolphin
    - *L. acutus*, Atlantic white-sided dolphin
    - *L. albirostris*, White-beaked dolphin
- Genus : *Lagenodelphis*
  - Species : *L. hosei*, Fraser's dolphin
- Genus : *Delphinus*
  - Species : *D. delphis*, Common dolphin
- Genus : *Stenella*
  - Species : *S. attenuata*, Spotted dolphin
    - *S. plagiodon*, Atlantic spotted dolphin
    - *S. coeruleoalba*, Striped dolphin
    - *S. longirostris*, Spinner dolphin
    - *S. clymene*, Clymene dolphin
- Genus : *Tursiops*
  - Species : *T. truncatus*, Bottlenose dolphin

- Genus : *Grampius*
  - Species : *G. griseus*, Risso's dolphin
- Genus : *Lissodelphis*
  - Species : *L. peronii*, Southern right whale dolphin
    - *L. borealis*, Northern right whale dolphin
- Genus : *Cephalorhynchus*
  - Species : *C. hectori*, Hector's dolphin
    - *C. heavisidii*, Heaviside dolphin
    - *C. eutropia*, Chilean dolphin
    - *C. commersoni*, Commerson's dolphin
- Genus : *Globicephala*
  - Species : *G. melaena*, Long-finned pilot whale
    - *G. macrorhynchus*, Short-finned pilot whale
- Genus : *Orcinus*
  - Species : *O. orca*, Killer whale
- Genus : *Pseudorca*
  - Species : *P. crassidens*, False killer whale
- Genus : *Feresa*
  - Species : *F. attenuata*, Pygmy killer whale
- Genus : *Peponocephala*
  - Species : *P. electra*, Melon-headed whale

Family : *Phocoenidae* (Porpoises)

- Genus : *Phocoena*
  - Species : *P. phocoena*, Harbor porpoise
    - *P. spinipinnis*, Burmeister's porpoise
    - *P. dioptrica*, Spectacled porpoise
    - *P. sinus*, Vaquita
- Genus : *Neophocoena*
  - Species : *N. phocoenoides*, Finless porpoise
- Genus : *Phocoenoidae*
  - Species : *P. dalli*, Dall's porpoise

The zeuglodon, or basilaurus, a serpentiform animal. It is the best-known *Archeoceti* and probably the ancestor of today's cetaceans.

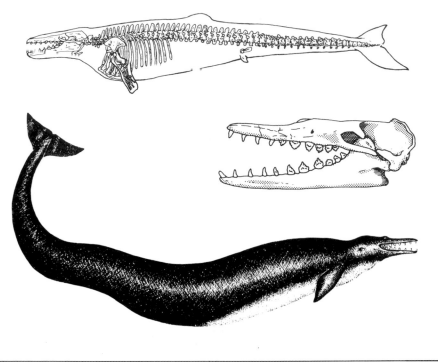

The oldest cetacean (or Archeoceti) fossils are approximately 50 million years old. One of these Archeoceti was the protocetus, an animal measuring approximately 8 ft. (2.5 m), whose fossils have been unearthed in Egypt. The balisaurus, or zeuglodon, which lived 38 to 45 million years ago, is the best-known and longest Archeocetan. It measured approximately 49 ft. (15 m) but could reach 69 ft. (21 m) and weighed at least 11,000 lbs. (5 metric tons). All Archeocetans had teeth. They disappeared approximately 38 million years ago and were replaced by the Odontoceti and Mysticeti. A great variety of fossils belonging to the Odontoceti cetaceans (Physeteridae, Squalodontidae, and Kentriodontidae) was found in 25-million year-old layers of soil. The Squalodontidae had sharp, triangular teeth with jagged edges and a wrinkled surface. These were small cetaceans that inhabited many of the seas and oceans of this planet between 25 and six million years ago. The Kentriodontidae were similar to our present-day dolphins, although they differ in certain details of the skull, which is quite primitive in these fossils. It is thought that branches of these animals evolved into the Pontopiidae, Delphinidae, Phocoenidae, Monodontidae, and Albiteonidae (now extinct) during the Miocene epoch, and then disappeared approximately five million years ago.

The Belgian researcher J. R. Laenen has suggested a new theory on cetacean origins, arguing that these aquatic mammals have too many teeth, vertebrae, and phalanges to be descended from land-dwelling animals. It is Laenen's belief that the ichthyosaurs (aquatic reptiles of the secondary epoch) are in fact the cetaceans' ancestors. This theory was expounded in a recent thesis, but the scientific community will need to consider it further before endorsing it.

Left: A group of Delphinus delphis. *Bottom. Examples of female (left) and male (right) dentition of Yangtze River dolphins.*

A LIVING TORPEDO

High-Performance Animals

Cetaceans are about 350 million years younger than fish. Nonetheless, their body shape is noticeably more sophisticated than that of most fish. As a result of their hydrodynamism, intelligence, ability to communicate, and extraordinary faculty of echolocation, dolphins are the masters of seas and oceans. The cetaceans' bodily morphology has changed during the course of evolution, endowing them with perfect ease in the marine environment. Various species are more or less hydrodynamic, and their body shape varies according to their predilections; thus, differences can be seen among migratory, pelagic (ocean-dwelling), and coastal animals. Within the Delphinidae family, there are both slender animals, such as the genera Stenella, Tursiops, and Delphinus, and stockier species, such as the killer and the pilot whales. The Phocoenidae are stocky animals, but this does not keep them from being quick and unobtrusive. Platanistidae have settled in rivers, and their bodies have undergone some changes, but they have retained the hydrodynamic quality that is essential to their dominion of our planet's major rivers.

In the late 1950s, a German hydrodynamist demonstrated that when a dolphin moves, the water resistance is 10 times lower than for an artificial, plastic-covered model of the same weight and shape. The cetacean's speed is not just due to its hydrodynamism but also to its skin structure that is both very smooth and very supple. It is composed of two basic layers, one superficial and elastic (epidermis) and one internal and supple (dermis). The dermis is characterized by a high papilla and a

Pacific white-sided dolphin (Lagenorhynchus obliquidens)

layer of fat. When the dolphin swims quickly, the small whirlpools that may form are isolated from the surrounding water and absorbed by the skin. This results in the laminar flow of the water over the animal's skin, which facilitates rapid movement. Pronounced differences within the dolphin's pigmentation on its flanks have been understood as subcutaneous reinforcements that channel the traction forces acting upon the skin. These colored lines represent the laminar flow's trajectory.

Each fin fulfills a specific role, and its placement on the body is necessary for the animal's balance and mobility. The dorsal fin's function is to stabilize the cetacean, like a keel on a boat. It exists in three basic shapes: falcate (hooked or curved like a sickle), triangular, and rounded off. A fourth type, which is specific to the adult male killer whale, is high and straight. The fin's morphology varies between the quick, pelagic species, in which it is falcate, and the coastal animals, in which it is rounded off, triangular, and also falcate. Some cetaceans have no dorsal fin (Lissodelphis), and others have a crest of varying length and height in its place (finless dolphin, beluga). The dorsal fin can also take an elongated shape (Platanistidae). The forelimbs have evolved into a pair of pectoral fins, or flippers, that help maintain balance and direction. Propulsion takes place due to the flukes, or caudal fin, which moves from top to bottom, as a result of powerful muscles lodged in the trunk and affixed to the bones by strong tendons. The cetacean's tail is horizontal with two symmetrical lobes. When the tail moves from top to bottom, its tips curve upwards as the movement is directed downwards. When the caudal fin moves

Tail Movements for Dolphin Propulsion
(from D. Van Heel, 1974)

In a slow-swimming dolphin, it is easy to see that the caudal fin is flat for the upward stroke and that the tips curve for the downward stroke. The tail's surface forms a more or less acute angle with the base, depending on the speed.

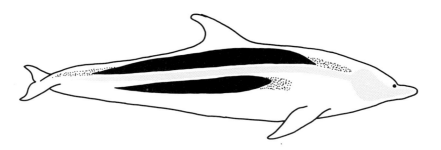

A muscle can only work by contraction; it is then extended by the action of an antagonistic muscle or by elastic tissue. It is clear that the upward stroke is much more powerful than the downward stroke, since the pair of muscles attached above the spine is twice as heavy as that attached below.

The Hydrodynamism of the Dolphin

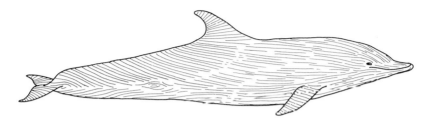

The subcutaneous reinforcements' disposition mirrors the laminar flow's supposed trajectory, according to the theory of Purves (from D. Van Heel, 1974).

Diagram of the laminar-flow movement on the dolphin (from D. Van Heel, 1974)

Diagram of the laminar flow (from A. Collet, 1987)

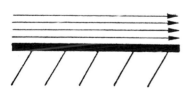

At slow speed, the flow on the skin is laminar.

At a higher speed, the laminar flow can be recuperated by the skin, which absorbs the small turbulences.

upwards, the tail's surface is flat. Thus, we know that it is only its top-to-bottom movement that provides propulsion, and that the bottom-to-top movement only serves to get it back in place for the next stroke.

Breathing

Cetaceans are marine animals with aerial respiration that, unlike fish, have no branchiae. They must come to the surface and oxygenate themselves through an orifice on top of their head called a blowhole, which is double in the Mysticeti and simple in the Odontoceti. In both cases, it is sealed by an external valve that the animal controls voluntarily and that prevents water from infiltrating the nasal passages.

The blowhole's opening is controlled by two muscles secured to the brain and to the valve, and its closing is controlled by a very efficient system of pneumatic cavities. The valve opens very quickly and essentially in two steps. While carbon dioxide is breathed out, the valve is only partly open and a small cloud of steam is visible escaping from the top of the animal's head. When the animal is breathing in and filling its lungs with fresh air, the valve is completely open. One can then hear a sort of sigh, which is barely audible in the Odontoceti and quite loud in whales and rorquals. Cetaceans renew almost 85 percent of their pulmonary capacity, as compared to 15 percent for man (55 percent in forced respiration). Since a single emersion is not sufficient for a complete ventilation of the lungs, cetaceans must surface many times in a row. The number of ventilations and thus the number of emersions (each emersion corresponds to a single ventilation) varies according to the length of the previous immersion, the an-

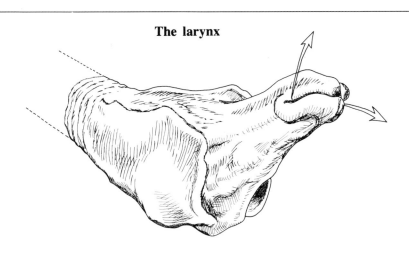

The larynx

The larynx forms a closed beak that prevents any water present in the nasal cavities form entering into the lungs. Air escapes through the two slits in the valve. The pressure exerted by the slits' lips allows the dolphin to produce sounds of varying acuteness, be they whistles, croakings, or gratings, somewhat like what we do when we whistle through our fingers. Cetaceans lack vocal cords.

ticipated length of the following immersion, and also the amount of physical effort supplied. The number of ventilations thus determines the following apnea's length.

The dolphins' larynx, a continuation of the trachea, is made of cartilaginous tubing and found at the intersection of the mouth cavity and the internal nasal conduit. It crosses the esophagus and extends into the internal nasal conduit and is closed by a pair of lips forming a perfectly waterproof seal. Thus, when the dolphin ingests its prey, the latter travels around the larynx and never comes into contact with the trachea, protecting the dolphin from the possibility of choking. On the other hand, the complete separation between the feeding and breathing systems prevents dolphins from breathing through their mouths.

Schematic rendering of the bottlenose dolphin's blowhole, tracheal artery, larynx, and esophagus (from D. Van Heel, 1974)

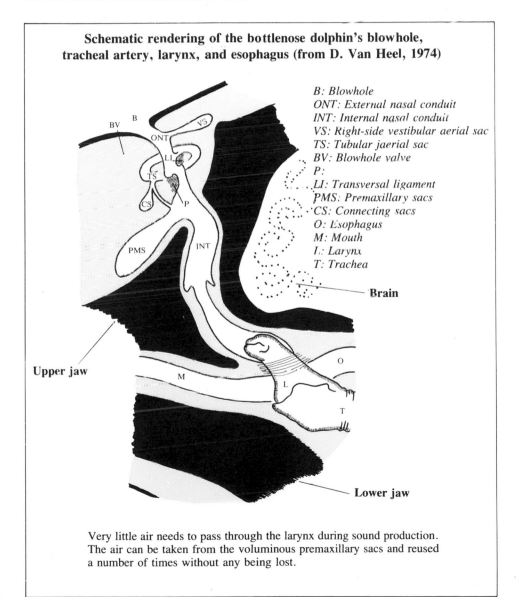

B: Blowhole
ONT: External nasal conduit
INT: Internal nasal conduit
VS: Right-side vestibular aerial sac
TS: Tubular jaerial sac
BV: Blowhole valve
P:
LI: Transversal ligament
PMS: Premaxillary sacs
CS: Connecting sacs
O: Esophagus
M: Mouth
L: Larynx
T: Trachea

Very little air needs to pass through the larynx during sound production. The air can be taken from the voluminous premaxillary sacs and reused a number of times without any being lost.

Sound Production

Cetaceans lack vocal cords; the sounds they emit are due to their respiratory system, especially their internal nasal conduit. Dolphins store air in three pairs of air sacks and use these sacs to produce sounds. When emitting sounds, the dolphin moves the air from one sac to the other, without any loss of air. The larynx also seems to play a role in sound emission. The air expelled from the pulmonary cavity towards the internal nasal conduit escapes through the lips of the larynx, which produces whistles, creaking, and clicks, depending on the intensity of the pressure exerted by the lips.

Sometimes large columns of bubbles rise above the dolphin's head when it emits long and powerful whistles. However, no air escapes through the valve during echolocation.

Two types of sound, each with a specific function, can be distinguished in the Odontoccti. They are either used for communication or caused by emotional situations (whistles, pulse bursts), or they are emitted for the purposes of orientation and environmental analysis (echolocation clicks).

The whistles, which are relatively pure sounds, occupy a narrow frequency range and can be modulated. Some researchers believe that the stereotypical aspect of each dolphin's whistles constitutes an acoustic "signature." Furthermore, recent works on killer whales and bottlenose dolphins have shown that each individual of a species has its own "voice" that belongs to it alone. It has also been noted that within a single species, each herd, or geographically determined population, has a slightly different acoustic structure for the same stereotypical sound. Some researchers go

The killer whale's powerful blow during emersion

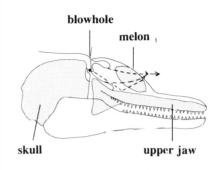

High-Frequency Sound Emission

blowhole

melon

skull

upper jaw

When the dolphin wants to know the object it is exploring precisely, it emits high-frequency sounds through its melon, which allows for unaltered sound transmission in the water.

so far as to consider these differences dialects. However, these sounds are analyzed differently by various researchers, preventing us from having a codified understanding of this communication system.

The explosive sounds, on the other hand, occupy a large frequency range and resemble barking, wails, and moanings. They are often associated with emotional behavior.

In the bottlenose dolphin, the whistles' frequency range extends from 4 kHz to 20 kHz (1 Hertz, or Hz, equals 1 cycle per second), while the explosive sounds have lower frequencies (from 20 Hz to 20 kHz) and are better perceived by the human ear.

The noisy and powerful echolocation clicks come from the production of sound impulses occupying a large frequency range. These sounds are reflected by the environment and allow the cetaceans to analyze it with greater or lesser detail according to the rate of emission. A high frequency, accompanied by a rapid rate of emitted sounds, is used when the animal wants to explore an object in detail. Inversely, low frequencies, which can travel farther and produce a larger electromagnetic wave, will provide the animal with more complete, but less detailed, information. The click's frequency varies from 200 to 300,000 Hz. This sonar (from *sound navigation ranging*) system allows dolphins to differentiate between two metals of different densities or between a dead and live fish. Due to hydrophones fixed onto dolphins' heads, it was possible to ascertain that the sounds they emit come from their fatty melon, which allows for the transmission of unaltered sounds through water.

Communication

In such a rich world of sounds as water, the dolphin has developed an impressive temporal lobe. Along with other cerebral areas, it is in a similar lobe in the so-called superior mammals' brains that sounds are emitted and analyzed and that the communication system is established. But in the dolphin, unlike in the monkey or in man, it has not been possible to demonstrate so categorically which are the motor or primary sensory areas, despite its well-developed cortex and other regions that are not yet very well understood. This neuroatomic support and rich sound environment have not been sufficient to allow for a codification that would underly a cetacean communication system. Different experiments geared to teaching a language similar to a human one have not resulted in the acquisition of a vocabulary or of significant phrases, or of the ability to manipulate concepts.

Part of our ignorance of cetacean communication comes from the fact that the sounds they use are very different from those in the rest of the animal world, and in ours. These sounds have also only been studied in captive animals. Nevertheless, it is apparent that dolphins have other methods of expressing themselves and communicating: Jumps, varied postures (body in "S" before a coupling, when faced with a threat, or feeling a strong

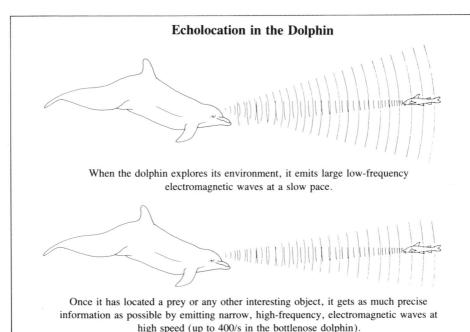

Echolocation in the Dolphin

When the dolphin explores its environment, it emits large low-frequency electromagnetic waves at a slow pace.

Once it has located a prey or any other interesting object, it gets as much precise information as possible by emitting narrow, high-frequency, electromagnetic waves at high speed (up to 400/s in the bottlenose dolphin).

emotion), mimicry, and ejections can all be signals of sensory alertness or of experiencing a critical situation.

The Senses

The sensory organs of cetaceans are well adapted to their aquatic environment.

HEARING. As mentioned earlier, the underwater environment is far from silent. There is a constant low-frequency background noise of up to 10 kHz, and the speed of sound is almost five times faster than in the air (1500 m/s vs. 330 m/s).

The dolphin has two receiving organs that are acoustically isolated from each other: the ears and the lower maxillary. The ears have no external lobes and are in fact two tiny holes on each side of the

animal's head, behind the eyes. Their main function is to assure a good perception of sounds at 20 kHz. In order to resist intense acoustic pressures, which are 60 times stronger in water than in the air, and simultaneously to allow for good sound reception, the massive ossicles are surrounded by highly developed foam-filled cavities, which isolates them from the rest of the skull and makes for a rigidity of the transmission system, favoring the passage of high frequencies. The internal ear has a tympanic membrane upon which the acoustic cells rest and that is much more rigid than that in earth-bound mammals. It also has a higher number of protoneurons, allowing for a better perception of high-frequency sounds and probably a better analysis of them.

To perceive echolocation clicks, the dolphin mostly uses its lower maxillary. The sound waves make the lower-front end

Cetacean Hearing (from D. Van Heel, 1974).

The ear.
A. In man, the ear bones, in which the cochlea and labyrinth are found, are where balance is maintained, and are an integral part of the skull.
B. Odontoceti and
C. Mystacoceti. The ear bones are suspended below the skull and surrounded by cavities filled with a foamy mucus that provides acoustic isolation from the other ear and from the skull.
D. The external auditory canal is supposedly open, but in fact it is blocked with cerumen and skin particles. The tympanic membrane is heavy and cone-shaped.
E. The auditory canal is open for a short distance and then changes into a string; it reopens further but is blocked by an auditory cone, formed by a tympanic membrane that is shaped like a finger pointing outwards.

Cetacean Ear (from A. Tomiline, 1974).

1 external auditory orifice, 2 layer of subcutaneous lard, 3 external auditory canal and its ossified area, 4 conjunctive tissue, 5 tympanic membrane, 6 auditory ossicles (hammer, anvil, and stirrup), 7 tympanic cavity, 8 tympanic bone, 9 petrosal bone, 10 foam-filled cavity, 11 cranial bones, 12 acoustic nerve, 13 stopper, 14 cochlea

Perceiving Echolocation Clicks

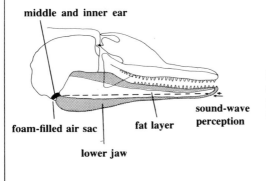

middle and inner ear

foam-filled air sac

lower jaw

fat layer

sound-wave perception

Sound waves are perceived through the tip of the lower jaw, and then sent to the tympanic bone and transmitted to the brain in the form of nervous impulses.

of its snout vibrate (through a thin layer of fat), and then they travel to the temporal bone before being forwarded to the brain in the form of nervous impulses. The brain receives all of the sound data and, after analyzing it, constructs an acoustic image of the general environment or a more detailed one focusing on a prey or obstacle.

TOUCH. Dolphins have a highly sophisticated sense of touch, and the cortical zones that receive tactile information from the skin are very developed. Dolphins are extremely sensitive to contact with objects and other animals, and they love being petted, especially on the tongue. Certain species have hair at the tip of the chin, on the border of the jaws, and around the blowhole. The dolphin's epidermis is very sensitive to violent knocks, strong lights, and dehydration, and it can easily be damaged.

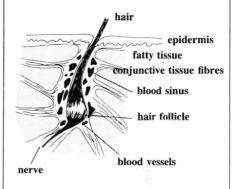

Schematic Rendering of the Skin, Showing the Cetaceans' Hair (from Fontaine, 1988).

These hairs are arranged in rows on the head. There are more of them in the Mysticeti than in the Odontoceti.

TASTE. Some structures on the dolphin's tongue are similar to our own taste buds. In studying the seventh and ninth pairs of cranial nerves and the area around the hypothalamus, which is linked to taste perception, it was discovered that dolphins are sensitive to certain chemical products. Taste is less well developed in the Odontoceti than in the Mysticeti. Although these animals are capable of swallowing sundry objects (balls, watches, and the like), they have been known to reject some food when held in captivity. This leads us to believe that they possess some faculty for gustatory discrimination, if not an even more sophisticated system of taste preferences.

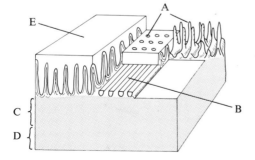

Dolphin Skin (from A. Tomiline, 1974).

A: dermis papilla
B: longitudinal epidermic partitions
C: subpapilliary dermic layer
D: subcutaneous fatty tissue and collagen fibre network
E: epidermis

The dolphin's skin is made of two layers: one, superficial and elastic (the epidermis) and the other, internal and underlying, that is supple (the dermis, which has a high papilla and a fat deposit). The epidermis bends and acts like a spring in response to water pressure.

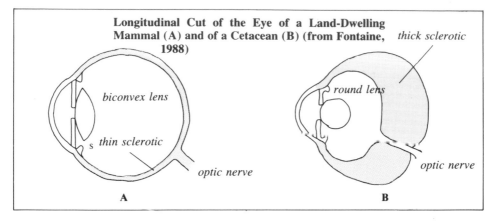

Longitudinal Cut of the Eye of a Land-Dwelling Mammal (A) and of a Cetacean (B) (from Fontaine, 1988)

thick sclerotic

biconvex lens

round lens

s *thin sclerotic*

optic nerve

optic nerve

A

B

SIGHT. Almost 80 percent of light is absorbed at a depth of 33 ft. (10 m) and 99 percent at 132 ft. (40 m). There is total darkness below 650 ft. (200 m). Thus, sight is not a particularly important sense in cetaceans, especially in the fluvial (river-dwelling) species and those that eat plankton or feed themselves at great depths. Marine dolphins use their sight to observe objects in close proximity; in the case of objects that are farther away, they use their sonar.

The fluvial species sometimes live in troubled waters and thus only use echolocation to direct or feed themselves. Their vision is therefore quite limited. Marine dolphins' eyes are adapted to both aquatic and aerial vision; nevertheless, they appear to be hypermetropic (far-sighted) in water and myopic (near-sighted) in the air, except for a cone-shaped area about 40° horizontally and 20° vertically in which they are exclusively hypermetropic (far-sighted). The Odontoceti's vision is essentially monocular, and since binocular vision is necessary to gain the impression of depth, the sonar system is all the more important. Finally, special glands secrete a

thick, gelatinous mucus that protects the eyes from the water's salinity.

SMELL. The parts of the brain concerned with olfactory data analysis are not particularly developed. For a long time it was believed that this sense was almost or even totally absent in the Odontoceti. But recent experiments conducted on three harbor porpoises published by a German zoologist, Günther Behrmann, prove the presence of a large number of chemoreceptive cells in the olfactory region, found in the melon's frontal and vestibular air sacs. Cetaceans' sense of smell is supposedly much less effective than that of land-dwelling mammals but could be similar to man's. The nasal orifice has evolved and relocated in 45 million years from the tip of the snout to the top of the head, and its principal function, smell, probably became secondary as echolocation developed and ultimately replaced it. Odors are detected around groups of cetaceans or isolated individuals encountered during emersion. Perhaps cetaceans analyze an air sample during their ventilation sequences and are then able to detect the presence of marine birds or man without using their sonar, or perhaps they analyze the state of another cetacean without using sound signals. Only further research will allow us to determine the importance of this sense to these animals.

Preceding pages: A group of bottlenose dolphins

Olfactory Area in the Common Porpoise
(from G. Behrmann, 1989

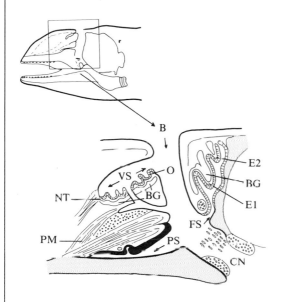

Schematic cut from the blowhole

B: blowhole orifice
BG: Bowman's gland
E: ethmoidal bone
FS: frontal sac
CN: internal nasal canal
NT: turbinate bones
PM: muscular plug
PS: premaxillary or inferior sac
VS: vestibulary or superior sac
O: olfactory epithelium

Olfactory Region in the Common
Porpoise
(from G. Behrmann)

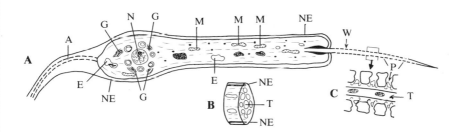

A. Olfactory cell model with a transversal section through the cell.
B. Longitudinal section through the olfactory cilia.
C. The olfactory cells are found in the olfactory epithelium.
A: axon
E: endoplasmic reticulum
G: vesicular golgi

M: mitochondria
N: nucleus
NE: nerve fibre
P: pore
T: tubula
W: olfactory cilia

Reproduction

The cetaceans' mode of reproduction is close to that of earth-bound mammals, and most notably man's. They are placental, viviparous mammals with internal fertilization Males and females are differentiated by size, male Odontocetl being larger. Males sometimes have a larger morphology than females, as is the case with the Globicephala, and their dorsal fin can be different, as with the Orcinus. The penis is held inside the body in a sheath and is curved in the form of an "S". Made of elastic tissues, it is indirectly attached to the pelvis's vestigial remains by muscles. During an erection, it comes out of its sheath and, due to its elasticity, quickly expands. The vagina is closed by skin folds that ensure waterproofness and extend outside the body, creating perfect conditions for the meeting of the gametes. The ovaries are found in the abdominal cavity, in dorsal position.

Courting behavior can be spectacular and lengthy, sometimes lasting for days, even weeks. Generally, the two partners swim together, fondling each other with their fins. The couplings are quite brief, lasting only one to two seconds, but they are repeated many times.

In earth-bound mammals, the length of gestation is usually related to the size of the animal. This is true of the Odontoceti but not of the Mysticeti. In the toothed cetaceans, gestation lasts from seven months (Dall's porpoise) to 16 months (pilot and killer whales) or even 17 months (northern berardius). Female cetaceans have a two-horned uterus; the fetus usually develops in the left horn, while the placenta takes up the right.

In all cetaceans, babies are generally born tail first, which seems logical since they are aerial-respiration animals and this helps prevent drowning; furthermore, as the newborn's head is the heaviest part of its body, it is lodged deeper in its mother's stomach. Nevertheless, there are births in which the baby appears headfirst. During

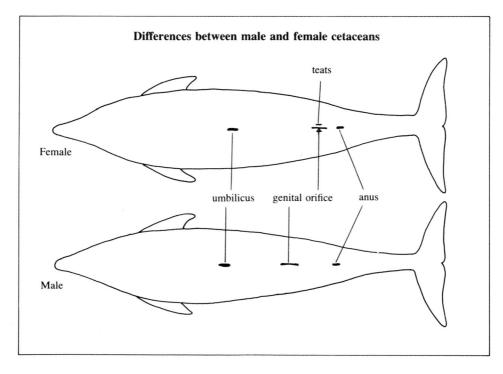

Differences between male and female cetaceans

teats

Female

umbilicus   genital orifice   anus

Male

birth, the baby's fins are positioned so as to avoid any risk of entanglement. The umbilical cord, which measures approximately 45 percent of the baby's total length, detaches itself by rupturing at the umbilicus level. As soon as the newborn leaves the uterus, it is guided, sometimes even pushed, towards the surface of the water by other adult females so that it can take its first breath of fresh air. Indeed, there is always a female, considered an "aunt" by the mother, that repeatedly directs the newborn towards the surface with its snout, as if it were conducting the baby's apprenticeship of apnea.

Newborns measure a third, sometimes even a half, of their mother's length. Immediately after birth, the baby searches for one of the two nipples found in skin folds on both sides of the genital slit. The milk is richer in calcium, phosphorus, fats, and proteins than that of land-dwelling mammals. This rich composition helps the young dolphin to grow rapidly and face the heat loss that is so much greater in water than on land. The milk, which has a creamy consistency, is injected into the infant's beak through the contraction of the mother's muscles. The nursing period is longer for the Odontoceti (12 to 14 months) than for the Mysticeti (five to 12 months).

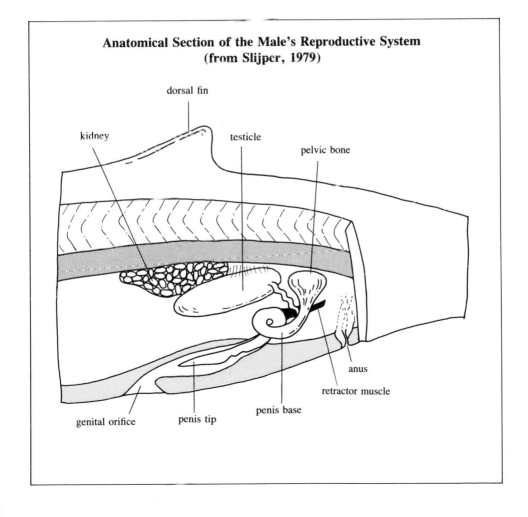

Anatomical Section of the Male's Reproductive System
(from Slijper, 1979)

dorsal fin

kidney

testicle

pelvic bone

anus

retractor muscle

genital orifice

penis tip

penis base

Birth of an Irrawaddy dolphin.

38

Feeding

Cetaceans do not chew their food; they swallow it whole, letting their muscular forestomach grind it. The Odontoceti's teeth are only used to seize prey and occasionally to rip meat apart (killer whale). In the ichthyophagous (feeding-on-fish) species, the teeth are long and numerous, whereas in the teutophagous cetaceans (that feed on cephalopods), the teeth are small and there are often few of them or vestigial ones, as in Risso's dolphin, which can only be felt at the edge of the skin.

The morphology of the teeth and snout influence the diet. For example, we find a short snout and a few spade-shaped teeth in species such as the beluga and the Phocoendae; the teeth are implanted in the jaw so as to function somewhat like a pair of scissors. Ichthyophagous species also eat cuttlefish and squid and generally swallow anything that comes along. The dolphin's diet varies not only according to its geographic location, but also according to the seasons and the availability of prey, both from a quantitative and qualitative point of view.

The killer whale, to cite another example, feeds just as well on cephalopods and fish as on marine mammals. Its menu varies according to its location as well as its social context. In British Columbia, Canada, for instance, two big groups of killer whales have been studied around the island of Vancouver: those in transit and the residents. The former travel around the island and attack marine mammals; the less-nomadic latter remain along the coast, mostly between the island and the American continent, and primarily feed on fish (salmon especially). Generally, fish and cephalopods constitute this animal's basic diet. They do occasionally attack a whale or a rorqual as a group, but it is primarily to eat the animal's fat, dorsal fin, and tongue. This is a far cry from the 13 harbor porpoises and 14 seals found in the stomach of a 24-ft. (7.5-m)-long killer whale examined by the naturalist Eschricht. However, these were probably fragmentary remains rather than whole animals.

Strandings

When cetaceans run aground, they are condemned to die if they are not immediately assisted. As soon as they find themselves on a strand, or shore, the animals' lungs are compressed against the ground by their own weight, which crushes the heart. The skin is sensitive to the slightest blow and, when directly exposed to the sun, can suffer a lot of damage, some of which is irreversible, such as parching. The cetaceans then become easy prey for any earthbound mammal, as well as for numerous germs, thus risking infection. This stranding phenomenon was recognized four centuries B.C. Aristotle wondered why these animals would come and strand themselves on solid ground. Two centuries later, Plutarch attributed these strandings to suicide attempts; the Roman Oppian thought that the cetacean returned to land when it felt itself reaching the end of its life.

There are three types of stranding: an isolated dead animal in an advanced state of decay that lands by chance on any type of coast; either an isolated animal or a mother accompanied by her young that may be sick or dying, taking refuge on a gently sloping shore or in sheltered bays; and finally the mass strandings (from two to about a hundred individuals) that take place on gently sloping shores. This last category particularly concerns some of the gregarious Odontoceti species, whereas the other two categories encompass all species.

The false killer whale's impressive dentition.

The mass strandings account for an important percentage of all the strandings in the Globicephala, Pseudorca, and Pepnocephala genera. This percentage is smaller in other Delphinidae. Most of the species involved in collective strandings are pelagic. Exactly why these animals come to die in groups on the beach is still not fully understood. As mentioned above, Plutarch likened them to collective suicide attempts. Are these mammals prey to depression? What is the cause of this strange behavior? One other theory is that, as they get older, dolphins search for an old route they knew at an earlier time and have since forgotten. The American animal psychologist Keller Breland has suggested that these animals, when they panic, lose all their reasoning abilities, going so far as to forget that they are aquatic mammals, and instinctively flee towards land. Could this explanation be valid for every species?

It has also been speculated that a flaw in the functioning of the echolocation system in the pelagic species could be the cause of these mass strandings. But faulty navigation skills would not suffice to explain these occurrences. According to the Canadian biologist E. Sergeant, echolocation does not play an important role in this behavior.

Another explanation has been suggested that implicates pathology, and more particularly parasitology: The presence of parasites in the sonar's receptive system could be disturbing the orientation system. Since pelagic species are usually gregarious, a parasite-infested leader could make a navigational error and thus lead to the stranding of the entire herd, or pod. However, biologists have not made any major discoveries in terms of parasites when examining the numerous cetaceans that have been stranded.

Yet another hypothesis is that these collective strandings are the result of behavior that is due to faulty information when faced with natural phenomena occurring occasionally or periodically in the marine environment, such as red tides, underwater seisms, volcanic eruptions, natural pollution by medusa, chemical pollution, different water levels, full moons, geomagnetism, and so on. The existence in the brain of receptors that are sensitive to magnetic fields has been proven in the bottlenose dolphin, the harbor porpoise, Cuvier's beaked whale, and the humpback whale. Pigeons exhibit the same phenomenon. The regular variation of magnetic fields allows the animals to orient themselves, and the destruction of this analytical system, be it caused by parasites, other forms of pathology, or the presence of magnetic abnormalities, could explain the size of the strandings in certain regions. The presence of an enemy (killer whale, man) could also push an entire herd towards the beach. Such was the case in Japan for the strandings of the Stenella and Tursiops or along the Faeroe Islands for those of the Globicephala.

The last hypothesis being suggested to explain this type of stranding results from a study on cetacean gregariousness and can be summed up as social behavior. When stranded, a cetacean could send out distress cries, which, when heard by other members of the herd, could draw them towards the beach in an attempt to rescue the animal in crisis. This behavior is called "epimelectic" assistance, and could be the reason that a sick or parasite-infested leader might unintentionally lead an entire herd to the shore. Or a sick individual, supported at the water's surface by its fellow cetaceans, might be taken to the beach in order to breathe, and the entire herd might accompany it to the shore. There is yet another unanswered question: Why don't the Mysticeti strand themselves in masses? Is the explanation to be found in the differences that separate these two suborders?

What should we do if faced with a mass stranding? In order to help these cetaceans, we must first analyze the environment and apply what is already known to the situation. First of all, we must alert the fire department, which has some of the necessary equipment at its disposal, and because it will know which other agencies are appropriate to contact. It is useful to evaluate the size of the stranded herd and its composition (adults or young), as well as the animals' weight, which can be determined by their size. A 6 ft. 6 in. (2 m) cetacean weighs about 220 lbs. (100 kg), one measuring 8 ft. (2.50 m) should weigh between 400 and 500 lbs. (180 and 230 kg), one measuring 11½ ft. (3.50 m) should weigh about 1,500 lbs. (700 kg), and one measuring 15 ft. (4.5 m) should weigh between 2,800 and 4,400 lbs. (1,300 to 2,000 kg). It is important to know the weight of the animals in order to prepare the contrivances to lift them and return them to the water.

One must then try to lay the animals on their stomachs, without pinning their flippers under their body. Cetaceans must never be pushed or pulled by their fins, but rather pushed on their sides, at the base of their dorsal fin. One can also attempt to clear the sand or water that may be in their blowhole, constantly wet their skin with a wet cloth, and even attempt to dig a canal and put them in it so that the next tide can draw them back. In any case, it is important to stay away from their tail to avoid the always possible snap movement. When faced with a mass stranding, it is recommended that as many people as possible act quickly and calmly, without further disturbing the animals, which are probably in a state of shock. As soon as there are enough people gathered for the task, it is important to try and return the greatest number of animals to the water as fast as possible.

THE SPECIES

1. GANGES RIVER DOLPHIN
Platanista gangetica
(Roxburgh, 1801)

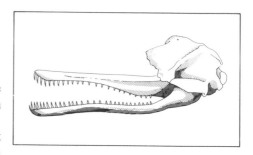

Taxonomy. During antiquity, Pliny the Elder had already been referring to a fish living in the Ganges that he named *platan ista*. But the Ganges River dolphin was not scientifically described until the nineteenth century.

Common names. France: Dauphin du Gange, Sousou. Great Britain: Ganges River dolphin, Ganges susu, Susu. Germany: Ganges delphin, Susu. Japan: Gangis Kawa iruka.

Description: The male Ganges River dolphin measures an average of 5 ft. (1.50 m) and a maximum of 6 ft. (1.80 m), and the female measures between 5 ft. 6 in. and 8 ft. (1.70 m and 2.40 m). Males weigh 70 to 90 lbs. (30 to 40 kg), and females weigh 90 to 180 lbs. (40 to 80 kg). Newborns measure 2 ft. 2 in. to 2 ft. 4 in. (65 to 70 cm). The adult has a dark grey back and lighter sides. The newborn is dark grey or dark pink. The snout measures approximately 7 in. (18 cm) but can reach 15 in. (40 cm) in the female; each side of both jaws sports 26 to 37 small, narrow, cone-shaped teeth. The little-developed dorsal fin is triangular and flattened, and it begins about two-thirds of the way down the animal's back. The pectoral fins are large, triangular, and indented. The flukes have a median notch. The eyes are very small and without a crystalline lens or epithelium.

Reproduction. The male Ganges River dolphin reaches sexual maturity upon measuring 5 ft. 6 in. (1.70 m), and the female, when she measures 5 ft. 6 in. to 6 ft. 6 in. (1.70 to 2 m). Mating takes place in the fall and spring. Gestation is thought to last eight to nine months, but it has been known to continue up to a year. The mother cares for her young for a year, but the baby seems capable of taking in foods other than milk at two months. Females give birth every other year. Life expectancy is estimated at about 30 years.

Population. The Ganges River dolphin's population is estimated at approximately 5,000, but this is an incomplete appraisal. As many as 300 to 400 are believed to live in India, and about 40 in Nepal. No estimation has been made for Bangladesh or Bhutan. Many factors threaten this dolphin, including pollution, dams, and poaching, which still occurs. In India and Nepal, it is hunted for its meat and oil; about 40 animals are captured

there every year, although it is a protected species in both countries.

Diet. The Ganges River dolphin mainly feeds on fish (catfish and carps), but it also eats crustaceans (shrimp and crab). A Ganges River dolphin in its natural habitat has been seen attacking a wild goose, and a captive one was seen eating a domesticated goose, which suggests that the bird is part of their diet.

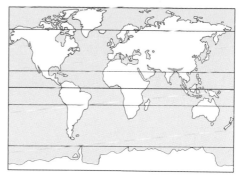

Field identification. The Ganges River dolphin emerges in three different ways to breathe: Either the melon appears alone above the water's surface; the top half of the head emerges above the water to the level of the upper jaw's teeth, followed by the dorsal fin; or the head appears entirely above the surface of the water, the animal dives, and the curve of its back appears while the animal sounds. Sometimes it jumps above the water. The dolphin remains immersed 30 to 45 seconds on an average and can stay three minutes without breathing. Underwater, it often swims on its side, the tip of its pectoral fin brushing against the bottom. It swims at a speed of 2–4 knots (3.7–7.4 km/hr) but can go more than 7–8 knots (13–15 km/hr). An

Indus River dolphin was observed swimming at a top speed of 16.8 mph (27 km/hr) and seemed to be far from its maximum capacity. It appears that the Ganges River dolphin swims at the same speed. Although it has a reputation for being solitary, it often swims in pairs, and there have been sightings of groups of six or more.

Communication—Sound emission.
This dolphin uses its sonar to direct itself since it lives in turbid waters with almost no visibility and has a very reduced optic nerve. It continually emits high-frequency sounds of 40 to 50 kHz, sometimes going all the way up to 380 kHz.

Distribution. The Ganges River dolphin is a fluvial cetacean; it lives in the Ganges, the Brahmaputra in Bangladesh, and in India. It has been proven that this species can tolerate a high rate of salinity.

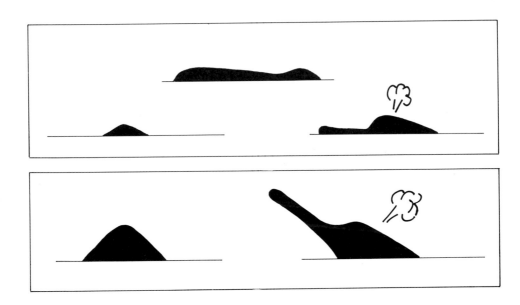

2. INDUS RIVER DOLPHIN

Platanista minor
Owen, 1853
or
Platanista indi
Blyth, 1859

Taxonomy. The skull of a dolphin from the Indus River was given to the British naturalist Owen in the nineteenth century. He was already aware of the Ganges River dolphin and found similarities between the two, but he considered the Indus River dolphin minor on the basis of its skull.

Common names. France: Dauphin de l'Indus. Great Britain: Indus River dolphin, Indus susu, Bulhan. Germany: Indusdelphin. Japan: Indus Kawa iruka.

Description. The two Platanista species differ in terms of their geographic distribution as well as their cranial morphology. For the rest of the description of the Indus River dolphin, refer to that for the Ganges River dolphin.

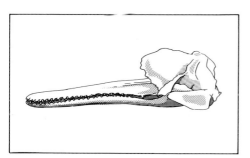

Reproduction. The Indus River dolphin appears to reach sexual maturity at the same time as the Ganges River dolphin. Its reproduction season begins in the spring, and gestation is evaluated at 10 to 12 months. The young are born in April and are breast-fed in shallow water (3–6 ft., or 1 to 2 m, deep) until the age of three months. The female gives birth approximately every two years. Life expectancy is probably the same as that for the Ganges River dolphin, that is, about 30 years.

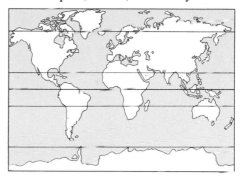

Population. This dolphin was indiscriminately and illegally hunted during the 1970s, which led it to the brink of extinction. Its population is estimated at present to be about 500. Most of them (429, according to a 1986 census) are found along 105 miles (170 km) of the river, between Guddur and the Sukkur dam.

Diet. The Indus River dolphin eats 4.5 to 6.5 lbs. (2 to 3 kg) of fish per day. According to the Pakistani, it also eats birds. As a result, the Djaber fishermen use live herons as bait when fishing for these dolphins.

Field identification. Refer to that for the Ganges River dolphin.

Communication—Sound emission. This dolphin's sound emissions have been studied in some depth by researchers at the Neurology Institute in Bern, Switzerland. These dolphins communicate among themselves by emitting sounds ranging in frequency from 800 Hz to 16 kHz. The sonar's frequency of emission is generally somewhere between 1 and 300 kHz. It emits between 10 and 1,000 clicks per minute.

Distribution. The Indus River dolphin lives only in the Indus and in Pakistan.

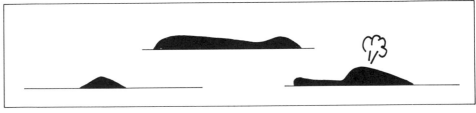

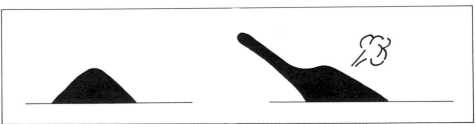

3. AMAZON RIVER DOLPHIN
Inia geoffrensis
(Blainville, 1817)

Taxonomy. In the 1790s, a Portuguese man collected the skull and a swatch of skin from a dolphin living in the Amazon River and brought them to the Lisbon museum. When Napoleon's troops occupied Portugal in 1807, the French naturalist Geoffroy took these precious samples back to France with him. Two of his contemporaries, the French scientists Cuvier and Blainville, took an interest in these anatomical pieces. Blainville described this dolphin under the Latin name *Delphinus geoffrensis,* which was later replaced by the genus name *Inia,* after the Bolivian Guarayo Indian name for this dolphin. Only one species is recognized, although some scientists have divided the *Inia* genus into two species or three subspecies.

Common names. France: Inia de Geoffroy, Boutou. Great Britain: Amazon River dolphin, Boutou. Germany: Amazonasdelphin, Butu, Bufeo. Japan: Amazon Kawa iruka.

Description. The Amazon River dolphin measures between 6 ft. 6 in. and 10 ft. (2 and 3 m), males being larger than females. The newborn measures between 2 ft. 2 in. and 2 ft. 6 in. (65 and 75 cm) and weighs between 15 and 18 lbs. (6.8 and 8.2 kg). On an average, adults weigh between 130 and 200 lbs. (60 and 90 kg) but may be heavier. The animal's coloring varies according to both its environment and its age. The young are a dark blue-grey with a lighter-colored stomach, whereas adults are lighter, usually with a grey back blending into a pink stomach. Some individuals are completely pink! The head is characterized by a long snout sporting sensitive hairs. On each side of the jaws, there are 24 to 30 teeth; the number of teeth appears to vary with geographic location. The dorsal fin is less developed than in other Platanistidae; it is only slightly raised, and runs along most of the back. The flukes

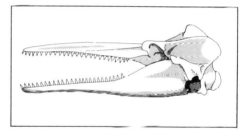

and flippers are rather large and extended. The eyes are small but functional.

Reproduction. The Amazon River dolphin's reproductive cycle appears to vary according to the animal's geographic location. Males generally attain sexual maturity when they measure between 7 ft. 2 in. and 7 ft. 6 in. (2.20 and 2.30 m); females, when they measure between 5 ft. 7 in. and 5 ft. 10 in. (1.70 and 1.80 m) or 3 ft. 3 in. (1.30) in central Amazonia. Gestation is thought to last about 10 months (though some lasting from nine to 12 months have

been described), and births occur from July to September (June to August in central Amazonia). Life expectancy is unknown, but one individual lived more than 16 years in captivity.

Population. The Amazon River dolphin is a species that is said to be common throughout the Amazon basin, though less so than the tucuxi dolphin, a cetacean that shares the same environmental conditions. There is no exact estimate of its population, but its density in the Amazon basin is thought to be one couple per one square kilometre of the river. This dolphin is threatened on many fronts, whether by fishermen, hydroelectric development, intensive forest exploitation, or both industrial and agricultural pollution.

Diet. This is a piscivorous (ichthyophagous) species, whose diet includes more than 50 different species of fish (mostly Characidae, including the famous piranha and silurids). It often adds a few nematodes and crabs from the muddy river bottom to its diet. It can usually swallow fish measuring 4 to 8 in. (10 to 20 cm). In captivity, however— more precisely in the Duisburg Zoo—these dolphins (from the Orinoco River) swallow carps measuring 8 to 12 in. (20 to 30 cm) and eat between 5.7 and 9.5 lbs. (2.6 and 4.3 kgs) a day.

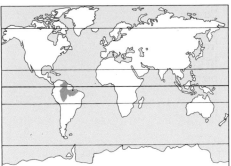

Field identification. The Amazon River dolphin surfaces every 30 or 40 seconds and can remain immersed more than 110 seconds (the record being 112 seconds). Its breath is noisy and quite high for a dolphin, at over 5 ft. 10 in. (1.80 m). Most of the time, when it emerges, only the melon is visible above the water line, and then the back, which the animal arches before returning underwater; the tail does not appear above water level. Some individuals have been observed jumping out of the water. It swims at an average speed of 2 to 3 knots (3.7 to 5.5 km/hr) but can push to a top speed of 10 knots (18.5 km/hr). It swims alone or in groups of two or three. This dolphin is renowned for its curiosity around boats.

Communication—Sound emission. Since it lives in turbid waters, the Amazon River dolphin uses its sonar for direction and in its search for food. Its sound emissions have been the object of

acoustic studies in the United States and Europe. The dolphin emits simple and multiple clicks for echolocation, ranging from 25 to 200 kHz. It also emits lower-frequency sounds, probably for purposes of communication.

Distribution. This dolphin lives in all of the tributary rivers of the Amazon basin and of the Orinoco. There are three different geographic variations: one, living in the north, in the Orinoco, Atabapo, and Temi rivers; another, living in the middle of the Amazon, in Peru and Brazil; and the last, the southern one, called the Bolivian dolphin, which is mostly found in the River Beni.

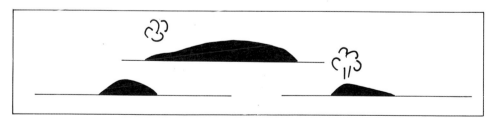

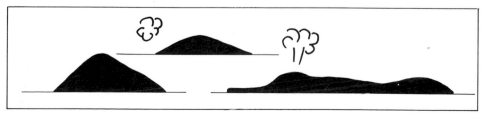

4. FRANCISCANA DOLPHIN
Pontoporia blainvillei
(Gervais and d'Orbigny, 1844)

Taxonomy. In 1842, Dr. Fréminger, a French naval officer, caught a dolphin at the mouth of the Rio de la Plata, near Montevideo, and brought its head back to Paris. The French naturalists Gervais and d'Orbigny described the new species and named it for the zoologist Blainville in 1844, naming it *Delphinus blainvillei*. The British naturalist Gray later created a new genus from the Greek words *pontos,* for sea, and *poros,* for passenger, trip, or crossing, as it is the only dolphin within the Platanista family to travel between fresh and salt water.

Common names. France: Franciscain. Great Britain: La Plata River dolphin, Franciscana. Spain: Franciscana. Germany: La Plata delphin, Franciscana. Japan: La Pulata Kawa iruka.

Description. Male franciscana dolphins measure approximately 5 ft. (1.50 m), and females measure about 5 ft. 2 in. (1.60 m); the maximum size for both is about 5 ft. 10 in. (1.80 m). The newborn measures 2 ft. 3 in. to 2 ft. 9 in. (70 to 88 cm) and weighs between 15.5 and 17.5 lbs. (7 and 8 kg). Adult males weigh approximately 80 lbs. (36 kg), and females 100 lbs. (45 kg), with a maximum weight for both sexes of about 110 lbs. (50 kg). The dolphin has a bulky body and a small head, culminating in a long, thin snout. Young

dolphins have a similar body shape, but their snout is shorter. The upper and lower jaws both sport 50 to 60 thin, sharp teeth. In general, the back is pale brown with a lighter-colored stomach, although some individuals are completely white (hence, their nickname of "white ghosts," coined by South American fishermen). The species has a triangular dorsal fin in the mid-

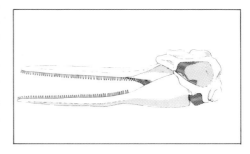

dle of its back. The pectoral fins, or flippers, are paddle-shaped, and the flukes have sharp extremities and a well-defined median notch.

Reproduction. The female gives birth to a single calf every two years. Sexual maturity is attained between two and three years of age, when the male measures approximately 4 ft. (1.30 m) and weighs between 55 and 65 lbs. (25 and 29 kg) and the female measures 4 ft. 6 in. (1.40 m) and weighs between 73 and 75 lbs. (33 to 34 kg). After what is believed to be a 10½ month gestation, the female gives birth between October and January. Lactation lasts nine months. The life span has been estimated at 15 to 20 years.

Population. Statistics regarding these dolphins are uncertain, and there is no estimate of their population. Over the last 30 years, a few hundred individuals have accidentally gotten caught in shark nets each year in Uruguay and Brazil. Between 1974 and 1985, at least 244 Plata River dolphins were captured in Uruguay. Since 1979, the number of accidental catches has diminished due to the decline in shark hunting in Uruguay. At least 723 dolphins were counted as having been captured in southern Brazil between 1976 and 1985. This dolphin does not seem to be particularly common, and South American cetologists are paying more and more attention to it so as to protect it better.

Diet. The franciscana dolphins eat at least 28 different species from the Brazilian and Uruguayan waters, including small benthic species of Scianidae. They also eat shrimp and cephalopods. Their diet varies with gender and age, as well as with the seasons.

Field identification. This is the only member of the Platanistidae family that lives in salt water. It is very unobtrusive, and there must be excellent meteorological conditions in order to observe it. It breathes every 30 to 40 seconds and can remain immersed for lengthy periods. It

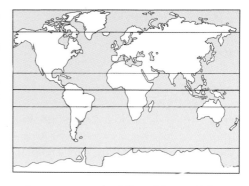

swims at a speed of 2 to 4 knots (3.7 to 7.4 km/hr) and occasionally precedes small boats. It is solitary but can move in small groups of three to five.

Communication—Sound emission. We have little data on the franciscana dolphin's echolocation capacities, but there is some discussion of capturing live specimens in order to study their sound emissions.

Distribution. The franciscana dolphin lives in shallow waters. It is a coastal species, found from the Valdes Peninsula and the de la Plata delta, in Argentina, to the Tropic of Capricorn, close to Rio de Janeiro, in Brazil. During the summer, it travels north and south along the Argentine and Uruguayan coasts, entering lagoons, but never going farther than 25 miles (40 km) from the shore.

5. BAIJI DOLPHIN
Lipotes vexillifer
Miller, 1918

Taxonomy. The Chinese were the first to describe this dolphin, in a work called *Er Ya,* which dates from the second century B.C. In the winter of 1914, an American named Charles M. Hoy shot a dolphin in Tung Ting Lake. The animal's skull and cervical vertebrae were sent to the United States, where they were examined and described by G. S. Miller in 1918. The name was coined from the Greek word *leipa,* meaning abandoned or forgotten, which referred to its status as an animal surviving in a small area of the world, and from the Latin word *vexillifer,* for standard-bearer, referring to its Chinese name (*Bai Ji,* or white flag).

Common names. Great Britain: Chinese River dolphin, White flag dolphin, Yangtze River dolphin. Germany: Chinesischer flussdelphin, Yangtse delphin, Beiji. China: Bai Ji Tun (pronounced Pei Chi Tun). Japan: Yosuko Kawa iruka.

Description. The Baiji dolphin measures between 6 ft. 6 in. and 8 ft. (2 and 2.40 m) and weighs between 155 and 200 lbs (70 and 90 kg)). The newborn measures approximately 2 ft. 6 in. (80 cm) and weighs about 11 lbs. (5 kg). The body of this species is usually stocky, and the snout is long, thin, and not too flattened, and tilts slightly upwards in front. The blow-

hole is to the left of the middle of the head. The pectoral fins are small and rounded at the tips. A low, triangular dorsal fin is found towards the middle of the body. The caudal fin is well developed and has a median notch. The eyes are very small and located very high on the head, whereas the tiny ear openings are found where other dolphins' eyes are usually placed. The animal's color is a pale smoked grey, veering

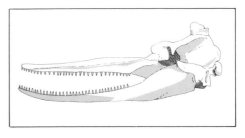

to white on the stomach. There is a white collar drawn behind the eyes. Each side of the upper and lower jaws sports 31 to 36 cone-shaped teeth.

Reproduction. Studies on the Baiji dolphin's reproduction are being conducted at the Hydrobiology Institute of the University of Wuhan in the People's Republic of China. This species engages in intense sexual activity twice a year, in the spring and fall. The female probably attains sexual maturity at the age of eight. Gestation is estimated at 10 to 11 months, and the young are born between February and April. The mother gives birth to a single offspring every other year. The life expectancy is estimated at 30 years.

Population. Approximately 300 of these dolphins have been counted, but the numbers seem to diminish yearly. It is said that their density is of one animal per 2.5 miles of the river. Although this cetacean has been protected by the Chinese government since 1975, many serious threats remain. For instance, it regularly gets caught by fishermen's hooks (this accounts for 5 percent of its mortality), there have been cases of collisions with boat propellers, and noise pollution, caused by river traffic, disturbs the dolphin's environment. It is considered to be an endangered species.

Diet. These dolphins mainly feed on small fish. Catfish remains have been found in their stomach, and they eat other types of fish as well as fresh-water shrimp. When in captivity, they eat the equivalent of 10 to 11 percent of their body weight every day. These dolphins gather in different areas of the river according to the seasons. Sometimes they come close to the shore and spend time in shallow waters near sand banks, in a detour of the river, or at its mouth. They eat early in the morning or during the night and can be seen jumping slightly above the water during these times.

Field identification. When in groups of two to four, they do not swim together, yet they surface at the same time. The young breathe more often and swim more actively than the adults. When it emerges to breathe, the Baiji dolphin splits the water

with only its melon and blowhole showing; then its dorsal fin appears and stays at the surface while the head immerses. The pectoral fins are sometimes seen, but the tail rarely emerges. The dolphin surfaces every 10 to 20 seconds, sometimes every 4 seconds. When in flight, it can remain underwater up to 135 seconds. The blow is only visible on cold winter mornings. This is a dolphin that avoids boats and ships and dives as soon as one comes near it. It moves in groups of two to 10, and sometimes up to 21. Single animals are also spotted. Its speed is estimated at 2 to 4 knots (3.7 to 7.4 km/hr). Mothers carry their young on their back or on one of their pectoral fins. These dolphins often rest on the river's surface. The percentage of time spent resting is higher in the summer and winter than in the spring and fall. They sometimes float on their back, exposing their stomach, for about 10 minutes at a stretch.

Communication—Sound emission.
The sounds this dolphin emits are classified into three categories: communication, echolocation, and sounds that are associated with certain emotions. When in captivity, this animal emits whistles and clicks. The whistles are lengthy, lasting on an average of 300 milliseconds, with an average frequency of 6 kHz. Clicks ranging from 8 to 120 kHz have been recorded in this species.

Distribution. The Baiji is 4,000 miles (6,300 km) long, and this dolphin is found

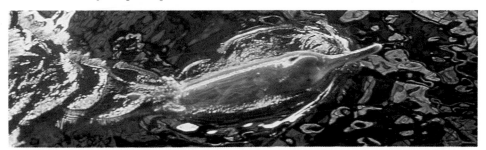

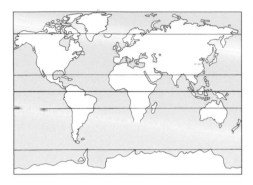

in 30 herds that gather in only 20 areas of the river, covering only 1,000 miles (1,600 km), between its mouth near Shanghai and the Three Gorges. Fishermen have never reported any dolphins in Tung Ting and Poyang lakes, although the first specimen captured by Western cetologists was from one of them. According to Chinese researchers, the animal's presence in that lake was accidental.

6. IRRAWADDY DOLPHIN
Orcaella brevirostris
Gray, 1866

Taxonomy. A skull from this species, collected in the Bay of Bengal, was taken to Great Britain in 1866 and subsequently examined by Gray. He described a new genus, from the diminutive for the Latin word *orca,* a sort of whale, and from the Latin words *brevis,* short, and *rostrum,* beak or snout. An isolated variety living in two lakes in southeastern Borneo without any contact with the sea has also been described. This type is supposedly larger than that described by Gray (8 ft. [2.5 m]) and supposedly has no visible teeth, although they can be felt through the skin. There currently is not enough information on this species for it to have a precise place in taxonomy.

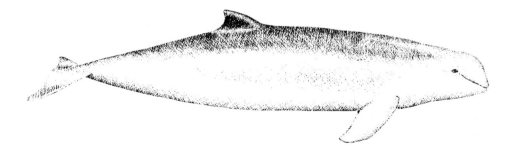

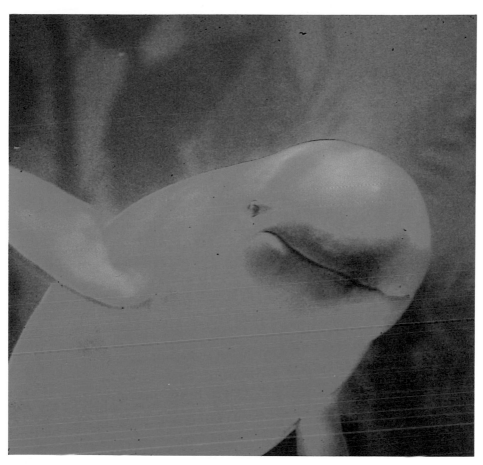

Common names. France: Dauphin de l'Irwaddy. Great Britain: Irrawaddy dolphin, Snubfin dolphin. Malaysia: Lumbalumba. Germany: Irrawaddy delphin. Japan: Kawa gondo.

Description. The Irrawaddy dolphin usually measures an average of 6 ft. 6 in. (2 m) and can reach 7 ft. 6 in. (2.3 m). Its weight hovers around 220 lbs. (100 kg). The newborn measures 2 ft. (65 cm) and weighs about 11 lbs. (5 kg). The body is long and tapers towards the ends. It has a marked bilateral asymmetry, with the right side better developed than the left. The animal has a distinct and functioning neck. The head is globular and rounded and only accounts for one-sixth of the animal's length. The blowhole is found towards the left, and the face is short and has no snout.

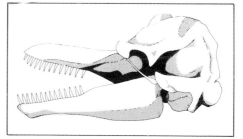

There are 15 to 17 teeth on each side of the upper jaw, while there are 12 to 14 on each side of the lower jaw. The dorsal fin is low and falcate, with a rounded tip. The flippers are short and moderately wide. The width of the flukes is about one-third of the animal's total length, and there is a well-defined median notch. The animal is blue, and it is a slightly lighter shade on the back.

Reproduction. We know little about the reproduction of this species. The mating season is between March and June in the Mekong. It is said that the cycle of sexual activities is directly linked to that of light. Accordingly, the Khmer fishermen see a number of couplings in the Mekong every day during April. In captivity, the Irrawaddy dolphin behaves similarly during this season. Gestation is thought to last 10 to 12 months, perhaps even 14. Females are believed to give birth to a single calf every year. Lactation is thought to last 20 months.

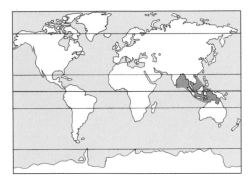

Population. This is a protected species and it is very common throughout its distribution area. It is sometimes accidentally caught in shark nets, north of the Great Barrier Reef off Australia. Its population in Chilka Lake in Orissa, on the east coast of India, has considerably diminished over the past 70 years. Nowadays, only 20 to 30 individuals have been counted in this region. As for the variety in southeast Borneo, the population is estimated at 200 to 300 individuals distributed in Jempang and Melintany lakes.

Diet. This dolphin feeds on small and medium-sized fish, such as carps or catfish, as well as on shrimp. Fishermen say it also feeds on the eggs and alevins of catfish (*Kriptopterus apogon*). At the Jaya-Ancol Aquarium in Jakarta, Indonesia, Irrawaddy dolphins consume between five and eight percent of their body weight daily, or 11 to 18 lbs. (5 to 8 kg).

Field identification. It is very difficult to observe this species when it surfaces to breathe. The melon first appears above water level, with the eyes remaining underwater; then the back, showing the dorsal fin, immediately follows. The flukes never come out of the water. Breath can be perceived from 330 ft. (100 m) away. The respiratory rhythm is quick: three breaths separated by 10 to 15 seconds, followed by an immersion of 30 to 60 seconds. This cetacean can dive and remain underwater for three to 12 minutes when it is scared. It can reach speeds of 12.5 to 15.5 mph. (20 to 25 km/hr). The Irrawaddy dolphin can be seen swimming alone, in small groups of three or four, or sometimes in larger groups encompassing up to 10 individuals. The Khmer fishermen, who have been able to observe this animal in its natural habitat, have reported that sometimes it holds itself straight up in the water and moves backwards, using its dorsal fin for support. They have also reported some animals blowing water out of their mouths up to 5 ft. away. They also say that mothers carry newborns on their back and use their pectorals to help support them.

Communication—Sound emission. This dolphin has not been the subject of any acoustic study, but it is quite possible that, due to its distribution in turbid waters, it emits high-frequency sounds such as those used in echolocation.

Distribution. This marine cetacean is found in coastal waters, estuaries, and rivers off the Indian Ocean, from the Bay of Bengal to the South China Sea, up to the north of Borneo. It swims in the Mekong, Ganges, Irrawaddy, and Brahmaputra rivers. It has also been sighted off northern Australia and Papua New Guinea.

7. ROUGH-TOOTHED DOLPHIN
Steno bredanensis
(Lesson, 1828)

Taxonomy. The skull of a dolphin of this species, stranded near Brest, France, was examined at the beginning of the nineteenth century by Cuvier. It was Gray who created the name of the genus in 1846 from the Greek word *steno,* narrow, and who named the species for the illustrator van Breda, who had done an excellent color representation of the Brest specimen.

Common names. France: Sténo rostré, Dauphin à bec étroit. Great Britain: Rough-toothed dolphin. Russia: Grenbezubyy del'fin. Latin America: Delfin de pico largo. Germany: Rauhzahndelphin. Japan: Shiwaha iruka.

Description. The rough-toothed dolphin measures between 7 ft. 6 in. and 9 ft. (2.3 and 2.7 m) and weighs between 285 and 350 lbs. (130 and 160 kg). The newborn's length seems to be between 2 ft. 6 in. and 2 ft. 9 in. (80 and 90 cm). The body is tapered, and there is no demarcation between the long, thin snout and the melon. Between 20 and 27 large cone-shaped teeth are set in each inferior and superior half-jaw. The dorsal fin is high and falcate and found in the middle of the back. The pectoral fins have a wide base. The caudal fin appears small in relation to the animal's body and has a deep median notch. The back, pectoral fins, caudal fin, and flanks are grey-black and studded with pink or white spots. The snout and stomach are white.

Reproduction. We have little data on the reproductive habits of this species. Both sexes attain sexual maturity as soon as they measure about 7 ft. 4 in. (2.25 m). It appears that, on Africa's Atlantic coast, midsummer is the birth season. The Japanese have had a birth in captivity, and a female rough-toothed dolphin gave birth to a hybrid in October, 1971, in Hawaii's Sea Life Park. The hybrid had a bottlenose dolphin (*Tursiops truncatus*) for a father and lived for at least five years.

Population. This species is deliberately hunted off St. Vincent in the Caribbean and both deliberately and accidentally off the shores of Japan. A small number are accidentally caught in tuna nets in the eastern tropical Pacific. Little data exists on this dolphin, but it does not appear to be as rare as was thought a few decades ago.

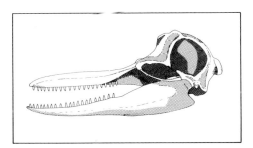

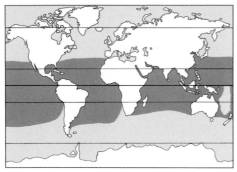

Diet. Fish and mollusks have been found in the stomach of rough-toothed dolphins that come from the Pacific Ocean. Pelagic cuttlefish have been found in various specimens from the Gulf of Mexico and off Florida, and squid in those from off the coast of Africa.

Field identification. This dolphin slices through water with its melon and dorsal fin visible. It emerges every 7 to 10 seconds, and it can remain many minutes in immersion. It can reach a speed of 15 knots (28 km/hr) and is supposedly attracted by the bow waves of fast ships, with which it likes to race. This is a gregarious dolphin that moves in packs of three to eight, sometimes even 10 to 20. More rarely, herds of 50 to many hundreds of animals

have been sighted. Morzer Bruyns mentions a certain type of rough-toothed dolphin, Elliot's dolphin (*Steno perniger*), that lives in the Indian Ocean and the Gulf of Oman, which supposedly moves in groups of 100 to 1,000, the average number being 300. The rough-toothed dolphin travels in the company of tuna and around herds of bottlenose dolphins, spotted dolphins, spinner dolphins, and the short-finned pilot whale. Mass strandings have been recorded in Senegal in 1948 (about 100 dolphins) and in 1969, as well as in Florida (1961) and Hawaii (1976, with 17 animals).

Communication—Sound emission. Some of these animals, when held in captivity, have been the object of acoustical studies. Clicks have been recorded with a frequency of 208 kHz, one of the highest frequencies recorded in a cetacean.

Distribution. There have been mass strandings of these dolphins, and their presence has been reported in all warm waters, both tropical and subtropical, of the Atlantic, Pacific, and Indian oceans. The rough-toothed dolphin is a deep-water dolphin frequently found at the edge of the continental shelf.

8. INDO-PACIFIC HUMPBACK DOLPHIN
Sousa chinensis
(Osbeck, 1757)

Taxonomy. P. Osbeck first mentioned this white dolphin from the China Sea in 1757 and then again in 1765. Later, different naturalists classified it from one genus to the next, until it was definitely placed in the *Sousa* genus. Three subspecies have been described: *Sousa chinensis* (Osbeck, 1765), the white dolphin (including the Borneo form); *S.c. lentiginosa* (Owen, 1866), the spotted kind; and *S.c. plumbea*, the dark variety.

Common names. France: Sousa Pacifique (or du Pacifique). Great Britain: Indo-Pacific humpback dolphin. Germany: Indopazifischer buckeldelphin. Japan: Shina usuiro iruka, Borneo usuiro iruka, Indo usuiro iruka.

Description. The Indo-Pacific humpback dolphin measures on an average 6 ft. 6 in. (2 m) but can reach 10 ft. 6 in. (3.2 m). Its average weight is 185 lbs. (85 kg), with a maximum of 305 lbs. (139 kg). It measures about 2 ft. 9 in. (90 cm) and weighs 55 lbs. (25 kg) at birth (in the China Sea, the newborn's length is 3 ft. 3 in. to 3 ft. 6 in., or 100 to 110 cm). Bodily morphology varies with the animal's age. The young have the same shape as young bottlenose dolphins (*Tursiops truncatus*). It has been noticed in the populations of western Indonesia that, in aging, a greasy tissue resembling a bump in front of the

dorsal fin grows on the back. By the caudal fin, there is a careen on the ventral and dorsal sides. The animal's snout is rather slender. There are between 32 and 37 small cone-shaped teeth on each side of the upper jaw, and 32 to 34 on each side of the lower jaw. The dorsal fin is triangular and located in the middle of the back. The pectorals are short and paddle-shaped, and the caudal fin is well developed and has a median notch. Coloring varies with age and geographic distribution, ranging from ivory-white with a white stomach to dark grey. Scars have been seen on older animals.

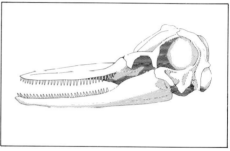

Reproduction. The Indo-Pacific humpback dolphin was studied in a project involving 16 specimens collected in the area surrounding Xiamen. The Chinese researchers discovered that the mating season takes place between May and June and that births occur between March and May, after a gestation period estimated at 10 to 11 months. However, it has been found that in areas to the north of the equator births take place between March and April, and in other regions births occur year-round, although at a peak rate during the summer months.

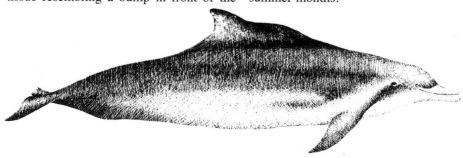

Population. A few Indo-Pacific hump-back dolphins are captured in the nets of fishermen in the Arabian Sea, the Red Sea, and the Persian Gulf, as well as in the waters of India and Bangladesh. Others are accidentally caught along the African and Australian (Queensland) coasts. This species is plentiful in the waters in which it lives.

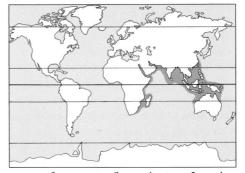

Diet. This dolphin feeds on various species of fish, mollusks, and crustaceans, which it catches in shallow waters (rocky areas, in proximity to reefs, and often among mangroves).

Field identification. When this dolphin emerges in order to breathe, the snout alone, or sometimes the entire head, first appears above water. The bump and dorsal fin emerge, and then the dolphin immediately puts its head back underwater, arches its back, and immerses completely. It stays between three and five seconds at the surface during each emersion. It surfaces many times in a row to breathe, and, before sounding, arches pronouncedly, showing its tail above the water; then it dives vertically to disappear below the waves for one to five minutes. It swims slowly, with a speed estimated at 2 to 6 knots (3.7 to 11 km/hr). This dolphin does not appear to fear ships, but it does not approach them either. When a ship moves towards a herd, the dolphins dive, disperse, and reassemble farther on. Some individuals have been seen holding themselves vertically with their head above water. Solitary individuals are occasionally sighted, but the species is generally gregarious and moves in groups of six to nine individuals, and sometimes up to 20. They sometimes swim on their side and the young jump out of the water. They have been known to travel with other cetaceans, such as the bottlenose dolphin and the finless porpoise.

Communication—Sound emission.
The Indo-Pacific humpback dolphin emits clicks and creakings with a frequency of up to 25 kHz. Whistlings have been recorded when it travels in groups.

Distribution. This is a coastal cetacean that spends most of its time in lagoons, estuaries, and mangrove swamps. It is rarely seen farther than 12.5 miles (20 km) from the coast. It is found in the area neighboring the Cape of Good Hope, along the west coast of Africa, to the Red Sea. Its distribution area covers the entire Indonesian archipelago and extends into Australia all the way to Sydney in the east and Carnarvon in the west. It is also found in the Canton River and one individual was caught in the Yangtze River, in China.

9. ATLANTIC HUMPBACK DOLPHIN

Sousa teuzii
(Kükenthal, 1892)

Taxonomy. In 1892, E. Teusz collected a dolphin skull in Cameroon and sent it to the Jena museum in Germany so that it could be examined by the naturalist W. Kükenthal, who claimed this was a new species and named it for its discoverer.

Common names: France: Dauphin de Teüsz, Sousa atlantique (or de l'Atlantique). Great Britain: Atlantic humpback dolphin, Cameroon dolphin. Germany: Atlatischer buckeldelphin. Japan: Africa usuiro iruka.

Description. The Atlantic humpback dolphin measures approximately 6 ft. 6 in. (2 m) but can reach 8 ft. 2 in. (2.5 m). Its weight hovers around 220 lbs. (100 kg), with a maximum of 306 lbs. (139 kg). The body's morphology is identical to that of the Indo-Pacific humpback dolphin. Once again, we find a bump ahead of the dorsal fin and a careen on the ventral and dorsal sides by the caudal fin. It has 26 to 31 teeth covering each half of the upper and lower jaws. The dorsal fin is slightly falcate, the pectoral fins are small, and the flukes have a well defined median notch. The newborns are a creamy white, whereas the adults are whitish at the level of the dorsal fin and occasionally from the end of the snout to the tip of the tail. Their flanks are grey and their stomach is a paler shade of grey.

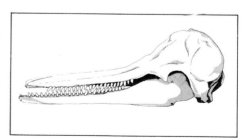

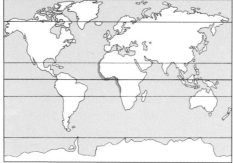

Reproduction. Little information exists on this topic. There does not appear to be a specific reproductive season for this cetacean, although a concentration of summer births has been reported.

Population. In Senegal, these dolphins are sometimes caught in shark nets. In Mauritania, the people take advantage of the presence of these dolphins by hitting the water with sticks to catch mullets. They are quite numerous in regions where they live.

Diet. Some mangrove plants have been found in the stomach of an Atlantic hump-back dolphin, but this was almost certainly an accidental ingestion. This animal mostly feeds on fish such as mullet.

Field identification. When it emerges, it behaves in the same manner as the Indo-Pacific humpback dolphin: The snout appears first (if it is resurfacing after a long submersion), and then the head and back come out of the water. It stays immersed up to three minutes. It can move alone but is often found in groups of five or six, sometimes even 20. Its cruising speed is 2 knots (3.7 km/hr) and can reach 6 knots (11 km/hr).

Communication—Sound emission. No research on this subject has been published about this species.

Distribution. This cetacean is found along Africa's west coast, from Mauritania in the north to Angola in the south. It is a coastal dolphin that occasionally travels into rivers.

10. TUCUXI DOLPHIN
Sotalia fluviatilis
(Gervais, 1853)

Taxonomy. The first description of this species came from a piece of skin and a skull brought to Paris during the mid-nineteenth century from the upper Amazonian basin. The name comes from the Latin *fluviatilis,* for river. Many types of this species were described in the nineteenth century. Three subspecies remain: *Sotalia fluviatilis* (Gervais, 1853), living in the Amazon and its tributaries; *S. f. guianensis* (Van Beneden, 1875), from the Orinoco and adjacent areas; *S.f. bresiliensis* (Van Beneden, 1875), a coastal species found between the Amazon and Santos, in Brazil.

Common names. Great Britain: Estuarine dolphin, Tucuxi dolphin. Spain: Bufeo, Bufo, Bouto. Germany: Karibischer küstendelphin, Tucuxi, Sotalia. Japan: Kobito iruka, Shiro kobitu iruka, Cyairo kobito iruka, Brazilu usuiro iruka, Giana usuiro iruka.

Description. On an average, the tucuxi measures 4 ft. 6 in. (1.40 m), although it can reach 6 ft. 2 in. (1.9 m). Its weight varies between 70 and 80 lbs. (32 and 36 kg), with a maximum weight of 110 lbs. (50 kg). The newborn measures between 2 ft. 2 in. and 2 ft. 6 in. (68 and 79 cm). The adult's body is stocky and has a morphology identical to that of the bottlenose dolphin *(Tursiops truncatus)*, except that the snout is much less differentiated from the melon. This dolphin has a short snout with 26 to 35 teeth on both sides of each jaw. The dorsal fin is slightly triangular. The pectoral fins have a wide base, and the caudal fin is also large, with a pronounced median notch. Coloring varies with geographic location and the animal's age. The body is usually grey-brown, becoming progressively lighter on the sides and culminating in a creamy white on the stomach. A pinkish coloration is sometimes seen on the lower jaw and at the throat level. Tucuxi dolphins living in estuaries become paler as they age, whereas those

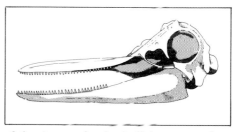

of the Amazonian basin lighten towards a creamy white. The young are black on the back and white on the stomach.

Reproduction. After a gestation estimated at 10 months, births take place in February and March, when the waters are at their highest level. For the Amazonian subspecies, sexual maturity is attained when the male measures 4 ft. 8 in. (148 cm) and the female measures 4 ft. 8 in. (146 cm).

Population. Tucuxi dolphins are sometimes caught along the coasts of Brazil and

Surinam in drift nets by the mouths of rivers. This dolphin is considered taboo by the native population, and certain parts of its anatomy are believed to be aphrodisiacs.

Diet. Small animals with a shell of some sort, such as armored catfish as well as certain crabs and shrimp, have been found in the stomach of these dolphins. This species has the right dentition for its eating habits and has been observed "chewing" its food so as to grind it before swallowing. There are plenty of other types of fish on which it feeds. When in captivity (observations made at the Duisburg Zoo), these animals eat an average of 5.5 to 6.5 lbs. (2.5 to 3 kg) of fish per day.

Field identification. When the tucuxi dolphin emerges, it does so rapidly. The

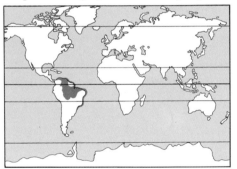

head appears first; then it arches its back and disappears immediately. The respiratory rhythm is one breath every 30 seconds, which is audible at a distance of 50 ft. (15 m). It occasionally remains immersed more than 80 seconds. This is a very fearful species. Sometimes it jumps out of the water to fall back on one of its flanks. Some individuals have been held in captivity in the United States since 1965, and 24 of them were transported to Europe. At the Anvers Zoo, it has been ob-

served that they swim alongside the bottlenose dolphins *(Tursiops truncatus)*, but they do show signs of aggressive behavior, so these meetings occur only under supervision. Tucuxi dolphins swim at a speed of 2 to 3 knots (3.7 to 5.5 km/hr) and can go as fast as 5 to 6 knots (9.25 to 11 km/hr). They move in small groups ranging from two to seven individuals, and sometimes even 20 or more.

Communication—Sound emission. These dolphins emit sounds for communication and echolocation through powerful and directional clicks.

Distribution. The three tucuxi dolphin subspecies are found in the entire Amazon basin and in its tributaries, along the coasts and in the rivers of Venezuela and the Guyanas, and along the Brazilian coast as far south as Sao Paulo. The tucuxi dolphins that live in rivers are smaller and lighter-colored than those living in the sea.

11. PEALE'S DOLPHIN
Lagenorhynchus australis
(Peale, 1848)

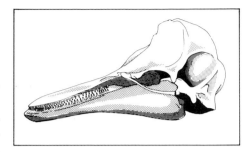

Taxonomy. The naturalist Peale observed two dolphins off Patagonia in 1839, and he drew them in 1848. In 1941, a specimen was collected and its skull was compared to that of another dolphin which had probably been collected during an American expedition between 1938 and 1942. This species had been observed a number of times at sea and, despite some cetologists' skepticism, still remains classified as a species of its own. Its name derives from the Greek *lagenos,* bottle or gourd, and *rhynchos,* for beak or nose, and from the Latin *australis,* south.

Common names. France: Dauphin à flancs blancs de Peale. Great Britain: Peale's dolphin, Blackchin dolphin. Germany: Süddelphin, Schwarzkinndelphin, Peales delphin. Latin America: Delfin austral, Llumpa. Japan: Minami kama iruka.

Description. Peale's dolphin measures an average of 6 ft. 6 in. (2 m) but can reach 8 ft. 6 in. (2.60 m). It weighs close to 240 lbs. (110 kg), with a maximum of 300 lbs. (136 kg). The snout is only slightly differentiated from the melon but somewhat more strongly than in other members of the *Lagenorhynchus* family. There are about 30 cone-shaped teeth on each side of both jaws. The dorsal fin is median, large, well defined, and falcate. The pectorals are small compared to the rest of the body. The caudal is very well developed and has a median notch. The dorsal area is black or dark grey, from the melon to the flukes, and the snout, from the eyes to its tip, is of a different black. The lower jaw is black and the throat is white. The flanks are light grey and the flippers are black. There is a demarcation in the shape of a black line between the eyes and the pectorals. A great black band before the dorsal fin stands out from the black back and runs towards the anus before reaching the flukes. A light grey band marks the flanks between the dorsal fin and the tail.

Reproduction. Newborns were sighted in the Strait of Magellan in January and February, 1984.

Population. In Chile, about 600 or 700 fishermen's boats use dolphin meat, including that of this species, for bait in as

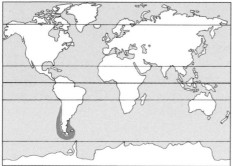

Identification. We have little data on this animal's behavior. Peale's dolphin is a gregarious dolphin that moves in groups of three or four, although groups of 30, and sometimes even 100, have been sighted. It comes close to ships and jumps acrobatically in front of them. It sometimes jumps close to small boats. It is known to swim with Risso's dolphin.

many as 30,000 crab traps when fishing for Royal Southern crabs. This probably constitutes a threat to the dolphin population. The situation is the same along the Argentinian coast. We know nothing about its actual population, but recent observations seem to indicate that this dolphin is common in the areas where it lives.

Communication—Sound emission. This dolphin emits clicks at a frequency between 3 and 5 kHz. No whistles or creakings have been recorded in this species.

Diet. Octopus was found in the stomach of a specimen collected off the Falkland Islands.

Distribution. Peale's dolphin is found in the coastal zones of lower South America and around the Falkland Islands.

12. HOURGLASS DOLPHIN
Lagenorhynchus cruciger
(Quoy and Gaimard, 1824)

Taxonomy. During the early nineteenth century, French research ships, with the French naturalists J. R. Quoy and J. P. Gaimard on board, found groups of black-and-white dolphins in the waters of Antarctica. The two naturalists called these cetaceans *Delphinus cruciger*, from the Latin *cruci*, cross, and *gero*, carry. Many years later, a skull belonging to one of these dolphins was brought back from Cape Horn; Gervais and Van Beneden classified it in the *Lagenorhynchus* genus.

Common names. Great Britain: Hourglass dolphin. Germany: Kreuzdelphin, Sanduhrdelphin. Japan: Dandara kama iruka.

Description. The hourglass dolphin measures 5 ft. 2 in. (1.60 m) on an average; a female measuring 5 ft. 9 in. (1.80 m) and weighing 250 lbs. (114 kg) was once captured. The average weight of the species hovers around 220 lbs. (100 kg). The body is sturdy with a short snout. There are about 28 small cone-shaped teeth on each side of the jaws. The dorsal fin is high, median, and falcate. The pectoral fins are long and falcate also. The flukes have a median notch. A black robe spreads along the dorsal area, and the lower flanks are also black. The ventral area is white, from the chin to the caudal peduncle. A white band stretches from the snout to the peduncle, cutting across the flanks and narrowing into a white line at the level of the dorsal fin. The dorsal fin, flippers, and flukes are black.

Reproduction. No data is available on this dolphin's reproduction.

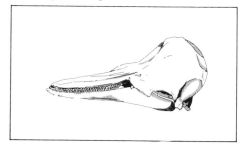

Population. We have very little information on this dolphin's numbers. According to certain sources, the hourglass dolphin is rather common in the Southern Hemisphere's colder waters.

Diet. This animal has been observed feeding on large fish.

Field identification. Hourglass dolphins usually swim in groups of two to four, although they are sometimes up to 40 strong, and regularly undulate. They swim before ships' bows and have been observed easily passing some, travelling at a speed of 12 knots (22 km/hr). They sometimes swim with rorquals, long-finned pilot whales, or bottlenose dolphins.

70

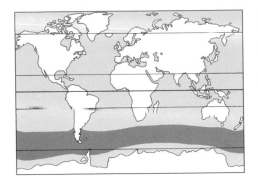

Communication—Sound emission.
This species has not been studied in terms of its sound emissions.

Distribution. The hourglass dolphin has a circumpolar distribution and stays in cold waters.

13. DUSKY DOLPHIN
Lagenorhynchus obscurus
(Gray, 1828)

Taxonomy. The dusky dolphin was described by Gray during the nineteenth century from a skull and a piece of skin of a dolphin from the Cape of Good Hope. The name is from the Latin *obscurus,* for dark or indistinct. Fitzroy's *Lagenorhynchus, L. fitzroyi* (Waterhouse, 1836), from South America, has been classified as a geographic variety of the dusky dolphin.

Common names. France: Lagenorhynque de Gray. Great Britain: Dusky dolphin. Japan: Harajiro kama iruka, Fitzroy kama iruka. Germany: Dunkler delphin.

Description. The dusky dolphin measures between 4 ft. 6 in. and 5 ft. 9 in.

(1.40 and 1.80 m) and can reach 6 ft. 6 in. (2 m). Its average weight is between 250 and 285 lbs. (115 and 130 kg), and the maximum is 305 lbs. (140 kg). The newborn measures 2 ft. (60 cm) and weighs 11 lbs. (5 kg). The adult's body is spindle-shaped. Its snout is short, not very distinct, and rounded. On each side of both jaws are 24 to 36 small cone-shaped teeth. The dorsal fin is median, falcate, and more vertical than in other species of the *Lagenorhynchus* genus. The pectorals are extended. The flukes are small when compared to the rest of the body and have a median notch. There is a dorsal careen, drawn from the dorsal fin to the tail. The coloring is generally dark grey on the back and white on the stomach, with a large grey area at the bottom of the flanks, extending from the snout's base or from the back of the eye to the anus. At the top of the flanks are light grey areas that run to-

wards the back, below the dorsal fin, and form two flames that cross above the anal region, culminating at the base of the caudal. The flukes, pectorals, and snout are dark grey. The lower half of the dorsal fin

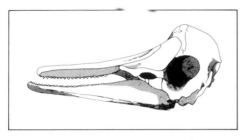

is dark grey, while the other half is light grey.

Reproduction. Female dusky dolphins attain sexual maturity when they reach 5 ft. 4 in. (1.65 m). Gestation is thought to last between nine and 11 months. In New Zealand, birth occurs during the austral winter (June to August); however, in Argentina, birth takes place during the summer months. Lactation lasts from 11 to 18 months. Females have a single baby every two to three years.

Population. Dusky dolphins accidentally get caught in Argentinian drift nets during October and November. They are also accidentally caught in the seine nets used for fishing anchovies and other fish in the southeast Atlantic. Some are fished by net or harpoon for human consumption in South Africa. A few specimens have been caught for aquariums in New Zealand and South Africa. This dolphin is common in the regions in which it lives.

Diet. This dolphin mostly feeds on pelagic fish, such as anchovies, and on octopus.

Field identification. The dusky dolphin is a quick and energetic swimmer. It sur-

faces four or five times per minute to breathe for five to 13 seconds. It stays immersed up to five minutes and can reach a depth of almost 500 ft. (150 m). It jumps out of the water when close to ships and accompanies them, easily following those going at a speed of 16 to 17 knots (29.5 to 32.5 km/hr). Dusky dolphins generally move in groups of three to 10, yet sometimes in bands up to 20 or even over 100. These cetaceans group by age. Along the coast of Argentina, the dusky dolphin's behavior changes from day to night: During the day it is active and looks for food, but once night falls it becomes lethargic. Some mass strandings of this species have been observed in New Zealand.

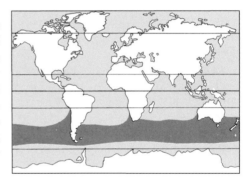

Communication—Sound emission. No data has been published on this topic.

Distribution. This is a coastal dolphin, found in the Southern Hemisphere around the Pole, in the cold and temperate waters of South America, South Africa, and New Zealand, to the south of Australia and the Kerguelen Islands. It migrates in Australia and New Zealand, travelling to the north of New Zealand in the fall (April) to mate and give birth and returning south with its offspring in October and November. In South Africa, it goes up to Walvis Bay in April and back down south in October and November.

14. PACIFIC WHITE-SIDED DOLPHIN
Lagenorhynchus obliquidens
(Gills, 1865)

Taxonomy. T. N. Gill of the Smithsonian Institution in Washington, D.C., classified three dolphin skulls coming from California as *L. obliquidens,* from the Latin *obliquus,* oblique, and *dens,* teeth. There are different geographic varieties, but at the present time only one is recognized.

Common names. France: Lagenorhynque de Gills. Great Britain: Pacific white-sided dolphin. Germany: Pazifischer weiseitendelphin. Russia: Tikhookacnskiy, Belobokii delfin. Japan: Kama iruka.

Description. This dolphin measures an average of 6 ft. 6 in. (2 m) and can reach 7 ft. 9 in. (2.40 m). Its weight hovers around 220 lbs. (100 kg), with a maximum of 300 lbs. (140 kg). The newborn measures between 2 ft. 6 in. and 3 ft. 3 in. (80 cm and 1 m) at a weight of about 33 lbs. (15 kg). The largest known newborn measured 3 ft. 6 in. (109 cm). The adult's body is fusiform (tapering towards each end). The short snout is only feebly differentiated from the rest of the body. There are 23 to 33 small cone-shaped teeth on each side of both jaws. The dorsal fin is median, large, and falcate, with a rounded edge. In the young, the dorsal fin is triangular and more pointed. In 1984, an old male, measuring 7 ft. 4 in. (2.26 m) and weighing 250 lbs. (113 kg), was observed in Japan. Its dorsal fin was huge and very extended on the back. Another individual with a dorsal fin similar in size and structure was captured in 1981. The pectoral fins of this species are small, and the well-developed tail has a median notch. The caudal peduncle is thin and heavily stocked. The body's coloring is dark grey and black on the back, while the stomach is white. There are light grey, oval-shaped marks on the flanks before the dorsal fin that extend all the way to the eyes, which are circled in black or grey. A thin, pale

grey stripe runs from below the eyes, crossing the body by going to the base of the pectoral fin to culminate, widening, in the anal region. Sometimes a pale grey flame shape is found in the lower region of the dorsal fin. The snout, pectoral fins, and

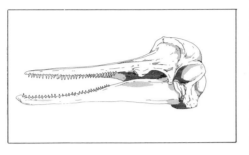

tail are black. The dorsal fin is black on the front and grey on the back.

Reproduction. Males attain sexual maturity when they measure 5 ft. 6 in. to 5 ft. 9 in. (1.70 to 1.80 m), and females when they reach 5 ft. 7 in. to 6 ft. 1 in. (1.75 to 1.86 m). Matings and births occur during the summer or in the beginning of fall. The length of gestation is estimated at nine to 12 months, with an average of 10.

Population. The population of this species in the northeastern Pacific is estimated to be between 30,000 and 50,000. The Pacific white-sided dolphin is caught by harpoon, and very often accidentally, in Japan. The Japanese have reported 241 animals caught in six years in various nets. Some of these animals have accidentally been captured in nets in the North Pacific. In California and Japan, some of them are caught to be kept in captivity.

Diet. This dolphin eats anchovies, hakes, herrings, sardines, and octopus (often *Loligo opalescens*). It eats approximately 20 lbs. (9 kg) per day.

Field identification. The Pacific white-sided dolphin is a fast and powerful swimmer. It swims at a speed of 12 knots (22.2 km/hr) and can hold this speed for 10 to 15 minutes. It can reach a top speed of 22 knots (40.7 km/hr). In order to breathe, it surfaces every 15 to 20 seconds. It is very gregarious and generally moves in herds 20 to 40 strong, although it has been seen in groups composed of up to 1,000. These dolphins separate into small groups of the same age and gender to feed. The herds include animals of all ages and both genders, and they have been seen travelling in the company of northern right whale dolphins, common dolphins, Dall's porpoises, short-finned pilot whales, humpback whales, common rorquals, and certain Pinniodae. This species jumps acrobatically above the water surface.

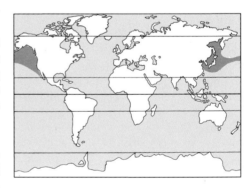

Communication—Sound emission. It emits clicks of a frequency of .06 to 80 kHz and whistles from 1 to 12 kHz.

Distribution. The Pacific white-sided dolphin is only found in the coastal waters of the North Pacific and the Bering Sea, particularly off California and Japan. It migrates to the north in the spring and to the south in the fall. It moves away from California in the summer and fall, travelling closer to the coast in the spring when the water is warmer.

15. ATLANTIC WHITE-SIDED DOLPHIN

Lagenorhynchus acutus
(Gray, 1828)

Taxonomy. This species first appeared in 1828, in an illustration of a dolphin skull from the Faeroe Islands. Gray named this dolphin *Delphinus acutus* from the Latin *acutus,* sharp, and, in 1846, classified it in the genus *Lagenorhynchus.*

Common names. Great Britain: Atlantic white-sided dolphin, Germany: Atlantischer weiseitendelphin. Japan: Taiseiyo kama iruka.

Description. This dolphin measures an average of 8 ft. (2.40 m) and a maximum of 10 ft. (3 m). Its average weight is 400 lbs. (190 kg), but it can reach 600 lbs. (270 kg). Newborns measure between 3 ft. 5 in. and 4 ft. (105 and 122 cm) and weigh about 77 lbs (35 kg). The adult's body is fusiform. The head is small and the relatively short snout is clearly differentiated. The median dorsal fin is high and falcate. The flippers are short, with an extended caudal sporting a median notch. The caudal peduncle has an upper and lower careen. There are 30 to 35 small cone-shaped teeth on each half-jaw. The back is black; the flanks are grey and have a white, oval stain extending beneath the dorsal fin to right above the anus. Above that, starting closer to the back than the flame, a yellowish longitudinal line extends to the base of the caudal fin. The eyes are ringed with a black stain that joins the black upper jaw. All of the fins are black. A grey band links the pectoral fins to the corner of the mouth. The lower jaw, chin, and stomach are white.

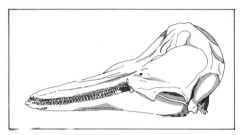

Reproduction. The female gives birth to a single offspring every two to three years. We know that, for males, puberty starts between the ages of four and six, but they do not take part in reproduction until they reach their physical maturity at the age of 10, when they measure 7 ft. 6 in. (2.30 m). Females attain full maturity at the age of nine (cases between the ages of five and eight have also been reported), when they measure 6 ft. 9 in. (2.10 m). Couplings take place in early fall. The length of gestation is between 10 and 12 months, and births take place in June and July. Life expectancy is of at least 27 years.

Population. The Atlantic white-sided dolphin is a common dolphin, at least near the coasts of Newfoundland and Norway. It is accidentally caught in mackerel nets in Cape Cod Bay as well as in the pilot whale hunts in Trinity Bay, Newfoundland. Hundreds of these dolphins are

caught in Norway every year by harpoon
and in nets. Forty-four of them were captured in the Faeroe Islands in 1976.

Diet. This cetacean feeds on fish, such
as herring, hake, and mackerel, as well as
on octopus and shrimp. A great number of
these dolphins swim into the Norwegian
fjords to catch herring.

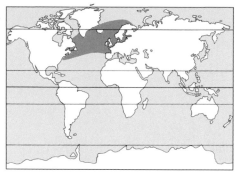

Field identification. The Atlantic white-
sided dolphin is a fast swimmer, often
travelling at a speed of 16 to 18 knots (29.5
to 33.5 km). It emerges in order to breathe
one or more times per minute. Only occasionally does it approach ships or come to
play in the waves of their bows. This is a
gregarious species, travelling in groups of
10 to 60 animals (which include all ages
and both genders) and sometimes joining in
a concentration of more than 1,000 animals. The groups are smaller in the summer
in coastal waters (six to eight animals) than
at sea (many hundreds). It has been reported that Norwegian fishermen once
drove 700 of these dolphins into a fjord in
a single take. This dolphin is subject to
mass strandings on the northeast American

coast; close to 200 were stranded in Lingleg
Cove in Maine in September, 1974. Herds
of these dolphins sometimes join with
bands of long-finned pilot whales, and they
have been seen feeding in the company of
rorquals.

Communication—Sound emission.
At present, we have no data on this topic
for this species.

Distribution. The Atlantic white-sided
dolphin is peculiar to the cold waters of the
North Atlantic Ocean. It is found along the
coasts of the United States, from the north
to the south, in the western Atlantic
Ocean, and up to the mouth of the Mediterranean Sea in the eastern Atlantic.

16. WHITE-BEAKED DOLPHIN

Lagenorhynchus albirostris
(Gray, 1846)

Taxonomy. Gray described this dolphin in 1846. The name comes from the Latin *albus,* white, and *rostrum,* beak or snout.

Common names. France: Dauphin à nez blanc. Great Britain: White-beaked dolphin. Germany: Weischnauzendelphin. Russia: Belorylyi delphin. Japan: Hanajiro kama iruka.

Description. The white-beaked dolphin's average length is 8 ft. 9 in. (2.70 m), and its maximum length is 10 ft. 4 in. (3.15 m). Its weight hovers around 500 lbs. (230 kg), with a maximum of 600 lbs. (275 kg). Newborns measure between 3 ft. 7 in. and 3 ft. 9 in. (114 and 120 cm) and weigh about 90 lbs. (40 kg). The adult's body is both sturdy and fusiform. The snout is quite distinct. The caudal peduncle of this species is careened but less accentuated than in the Atlantic white-side dolphin. The dorsal fin is median, falcate, and high. The pectoral fins are short and wide. The caudal has a median notch. Each side of both jaws has 22 to 28 small cone-shaped teeth. As a general rule, this animal's coloring is quite dark; the back,

pectoral, and caudal fins are almost blue-black. However, there is a whitish area on the back, behind the dorsal fin. A light

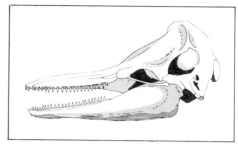

grey or white flame starts behind the eyes and extends onto the flanks all the way to the anal region. The snout, throat, and stomach are white.

Reproduction. This species reaches sexual maturity when it measures 6 ft. (1.90 m). Mating takes place during the warmer months, generally between June and September. Gestation is estimated at 10 months.

Population. The white-beaked dolphin is considered relatively abundant in its habitat, especially in the northeast Atlantic (in the North Sea up to Norway, off Great Britain's eastern coast, and around Iceland). Individuals are accidentally caught in the trawls of the North Sea, off Iceland and probably Ireland. Some are captured annually for fishing bait in Norway and Newfoundland.

Diet. This species feeds on common herring, cod, arctic cod, hake, mollusks and some benthic crustaceans.

Identification. A powerful swimmer, the white-beaked dolphin is occasionally seen swimming before the bows of ships travelling at speeds of 15 to 20 knots (18.7 to 37 km/hr). It does not go near small boats and rarely jumps out of the water. It moves in groups of six to 10, but herds of up to 1,500 have been seen. A single mass stranding has been recorded for this species, in March 1953, in Conception Bay, in Newfoundland.

Communication—Sound emission.
We have no data at present on this topic for this species.

Distribution. The white-beaked dolphin

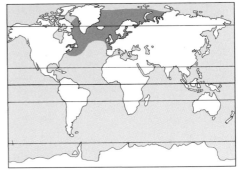

lives in the coastal waters of the North Atlantic, from Massachusetts to Iceland and Norway, and in the Baltic Sea, and in the North Sea to France. This dolphin migrates along the coasts of North America. In the winter, it is found swimming south to warmer waters off Cape Cod (certain individuals stay there until the beginning of spring and sometimes even throughout summer).

17. FRASER'S DOLPHIN
Lagenodelphis hosei
(Fraser, 1956)

Taxonomy. In 1956, the British cetologist F. C. Fraser described a new genus from a skeleton collected at the mouth of the Lutong River in Sarawak, on Borneo, and brought to London in 1895. Live dolphins of this species were observed in 1971 when 25 animals were captured off the Coco Islands (east tropical Pacific) and two others were captured in South Africa. The name is from the Greek *lagenos,* bottle, *delphis,* dolphin, and hosci, referring to C. Hose, who had found the original specimen.

Common names. France: Dauphin de Bornéo, Dauphin d'Hose. Great Britain: Fraser's dolphin, Short snout dolphin, Sarawak dolphin. Germany: Kurzschnabeldelphin, Frasers delphin. Japan: Sarawaku iruka. Russia: Sarawakskiy, Del'fin Frasera.

Description. Fraser's dolphin measures approximately 7 ft. 6 in. (2.30 m) and can reach 8 in. 6 in. (2.60 m). Its weight hovers between 140 and 185 lbs. (62 and 84 kg), with a maximum of 300 lbs. (136 kg). We do not know what its exact length is at birth, but based on the smallest specimen ever encountered, which measured 3 ft. 6 in. (1.10 m), it is believed that newborns must measure close to 3.3 ft. (1 m). The body is fusiform and stocky; it has pronounced top and bottom careens at the base of the caudal fin. The snout is very short and rounded. There are 40 to 44 small cone-shaped teeth on each side of the upper jaw and 39 to 44 on each side of the lower jaw. The dorsal fin is median, falcate, and small. The pectorals are small and thin, and the caudal, which is also small, has a median notch. The back is dark grey, and the stomach is white or a pinkish white. There are two parallel stripes on the flanks. The upper stripe, which is a creamy white, starts above and ahead of the eye and culminates by narrowing at the base of the tail. The lower stripe, which is black or dark grey, goes from the eye to the anus. There is also a black band between the mouth and the pectoral fins. The throat and chin are white, although the tip of the lower jaw is black. The upper jaw, the pectorals, the caudal, and the dorsal fin are black.

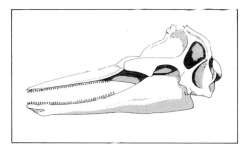

Reproduction. There is little data on the reproductive behavior of this species. A female measuring 7 ft. 4 in. (2.25 m) was identified as not having reached sexual maturity, but another female measuring 7 ft. 8 in. (2.36 m) was observed carrying a 4-

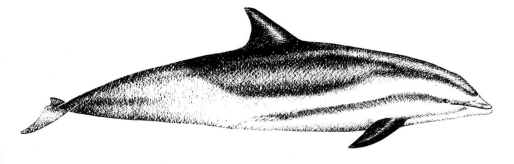

in.-long fetus (11 cm), which allows us to speculate that 7 ft. 6 in. (2.30 m) must be the length at which females attain sexual maturity. A newborn measuring 3 ft. 6 in. (110 cm) and weighing 42 lbs. (19.3 kg) was captured in the eastern Pacific in January 1971, and newborn sightings in February of the same year make us think that births take place during the austral summer.

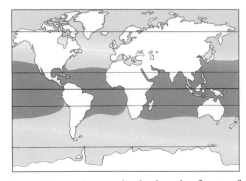

Population. Fraser's dolphin is thought to be common in the tropical and pelagic waters of the Pacific. Individuals are accidentally caught in tuna nets in the east central Pacific; as many as 7,800 animals are believed to have died in such a manner. In the east tropical Pacific, 60 dolphins of this species were spotted during a reconnaissance flight. Other specimens have been caught by a set net off the Japanese coast. Some have been captured in the Philippines for aquariums.

Diet. Mesopelagic fish (living at a depth of 650 to 3,300 ft., or 200 to 1,000 m), such as Sternoptychidae, Polyipnus sp., some Gonostomatidae, and Moridae, have been found in the stomach of Fraser's dolphins, which also eat octopus and crabs.

Field identification. Fraser's dolphins have an aggressive way of swimming, and they surround themselves with foam when surfacing. They are quick and sometimes jump out of the water, but these jumps are not as acrobatic as those of other pelagic dolphins. They generally avoid getting near ships in the Pacific, although this is not the case off South Africa, where they have been observed playing in front of ships' bows. This species has been seen in the company of herds of false killer whales, striped dolphins, spotted dolphins, spinner dolphins, and big sperm whales. Herd size varies from seven to eight individuals up to as many as 300 or 400. Some have even been seen that were 1,000 strong. In May 1984, a herd of about 30 Fraser's dolphins was seen in the estuary of Yaudy, in the north of France. The next day, 10 individuals were stranded on the island of Loaven. Mass strandings occur occasionally with these dolphins. There have been some in Victoria, Australia, and in Florida.

Communication—Sound emission. At present, we have no data on this topic for this species.

Distribution. Fraser's dolphin is uniformly distributed throughout the open sea in the Indian and Pacific oceans. Some have also been observed in the Atlantic Ocean at St. Vincent, off Florida, and in strandings, such as that of the 10 individuals off the Breton coast of France. This leads us to believe that Fraser's dolphin moves in colder waters than we previously thought and that its distribution is not yet totally understood.

18. COMMON DOLPHIN
Delphinus delphis
Linnaeus, 1758

Taxonomy. The common dolphin is the best-known dolphin of all times. The Greeks and Romans depicted it on their walls and vases. In 1758 Linnaeus described the species, from the Greek *delphis,* dolphin, and the suffix *innus,* which means resembling. There exist geographic variations of different colors and sizes, some of which have been categorized as species; however, for the sake of clarity, we will study only one species in this book.

Common names: Great Britain: Common dolphin, Saddleback dolphin, Whitebelly dolphin. Germany: Gewöhnlicher delphin. Russia: Obyknovennyy, Del'fin belobochka. Japan: Tobi iruka (adult), Ma iruka (young), Hase iruka (South Atlantic), Amerika ma iruka (North Pacific). Latin America: Delfin commun.

Description. The common dolphin measures 6 ft. 6 in. (2 m) on an average, with a maximum of 8 ft. 6 in. (2.60 m). Its weight varies between 200 and 300 lbs. (90 and 136 kg). The newborn measures between 2 ft. 5 in. and 3 ft. 1 in. (76 and 95 cm). The body is fusiform, long, and slender. The long, thin snout is distinct from the melon. The dorsal fin is median, falcate, and medium-sized. The pectoral fins are short, and the flukes have a pronounced median notch. There are on an average 40 to 50 small pointed teeth on each side of the two jaws. Coloring and snout length are the best ways to differentiate the geographic varieties. The common dolphin generally has a very dark, almost black, back. This coloration forms a sort of triangle, the lower point of which is found at the end of the dorsal fin. The throat and stomach are white or creamy white. Black stripes join the pectoral fins to the lower jaw and the eyes to the bottom of the mouth. On the front part of the flanks, there is a yellow pigmentation, which becomes greyer towards the back. One or two grey stripes run along the bottom of the flanks. The fins as well as the upper jaw are black or very dark, whereas the lower jaw is light.

Reproduction. The female common dolphin's complete reproductive cycle varies from 12 to 16 months, according to the

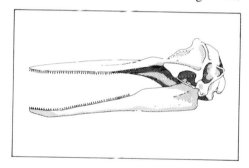

population. Sexual maturity is sometimes reached at two years of age, although it is usually between three and four, when the animals measure between 5 ft. 5 in. and 5 ft. 10 in. (1.67 and 1.80 m). Mating season also varies but is usually towards the

end of summer. Gestation lasts 10 to 11 months, and births occur in the spring and fall. Lactation lasts about four months, and the young are raised for one to three years. The life span is estimated at 25 to 30 years.

Population. The common dolphin is abundant in the Northern Hemisphere's temperate waters. It is impossible to estimate its worldwide population, but it is thought that at least 1.5 million individuals populate the eastern tropical Pacific. It is mostly in this area that hundreds of these animals are caught in fishing for tuna (in 1981, 1,400 individuals were reportedly caught). This interaction between dolphins and fisheries takes place throughout the world, notably in Japan and Turkey, but as many as 130,000 dolphins were reported to have been caught in the North Sea in a single year.

Diet. The common dolphin's diet is relatively varied. It feeds on gregarious and migratory fish, such as anchovies, herring, and sardines, as well as on octopus.

Field identification. The common dolphin emerges to breathe a number of times per minute, usually every 20 to 30 seconds. The longest recorded immersion of this species is five minutes 53 seconds (Napier Marineland, New Zealand). It is said to be able to remain submerged for eight minutes. It can dive to a depth of 900 ft. (280 m) and generally swims at a cruising speed of 3 to 5 knots (or 5.5 to 9.25 km/hr), although it can go over 25 knots (46 km/hr) when at top speed. When it emerges, it jumps in all sorts of ways, although sometimes only the melon and back appear. It plays with bow waves and often zigzags. It swims along with the striped dolphin. Very gregarious, the common dolphin moves in herds of 10 to 100, sometimes up to 3,000. A small group composed of a few dozen dolphins ventured into the Hudson River (New York State); two of them were beached, one 85 miles (135 km) and the other 170 miles (270 km) from the river's mouth. This dolphin is subject to some mass strandings.

Communication—Sound emission.
The common dolphin echolocates and emits sounds with a frequency of 100 to 150 kHz. The frequency range is of .2 to 150 kHz for clicks and of 4 to 16 kHz for whistles.

Distribution. This dolphin is found in the temperate and tropical waters of every ocean. Its migrations are directly related to those of the fish upon which it feeds.

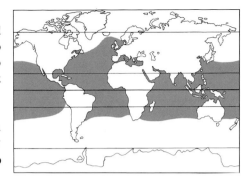

19. SPOTTED DOLPHIN
Stenella attenuata
(Gray, 1846)

Taxonomy. In the mid-nineteenth century, a spotted dolphin was caught at Cape Horn and described by Gray as belonging to the genus *Delphinus*. Later, a new genus, *Stenella,* was created from the Greek *stenos*, narrow, in reference to its long and narrow snout, and from the Latin *attenuatus,* reduced. There are a number of geographic varieties, differentiated by a few morphological characteristics (snout, fins, etc.) and especially by their coloring and markings (spots, stripes, etc.). These variants have often been raised to the level of specific species, but we will only keep to one species here. The following species are considered to be the same as *S. attenuata: S. graffmani, S. dubia, S. frontalis,* and *S. malayana.*

Common names. France: Dauphin bridé, Dauphin douteux. Great Britain:

Spotted dolphin, Bridled dolphin, Pantropical spotted dolphin. Latin America: Delfin machado, Delfin pintado, Tonino pintado. Russia: Pyatinistyy del'fin. Germany: Flecken delphin. Japan: Arari iruka, taiheiyo madara iruka, Malai suji iruka, Madara iruka.

Description. The spotted dolphin measures an average of 6 ft. 6 in. (2 m), but it can reach 8 ft. 6 in. (2.60 m). Its weight is usually about 220 lbs. (100 kg), but it is sometimes as high as 308 lbs. (140 kg). The average length of newborns is 2 ft. 7 in. to 2 ft. 9 in. (82 to 89 cm). The adult's body is thin but relatively stocky and fusiform. The snout is medium-sized and distinct from the head. There are between 41 and 45 small conc-shaped teeth on each side of both jaws. The dorsal fin is median, falcate, and thin. The pectoral fins are medium-sized, as are the flukes, which have a median notch. A careen is found under the caudal peduncle (sometimes above). Coloring is the primary criterion

for differentiating the geographic varieties. The back is generally a steel-grey, starting from the snout, going over the top of the eyes, and extending all the way to the flukes. The same coloring is found from the snout to the eyes, which it circles. The flanks and stomach are pale grey (sometimes with a pinkish tinge at the throat level). The pectoral fins are dark grey. A small area of the snout is white, as

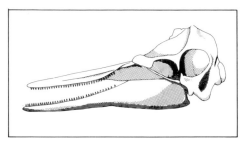

are the lips. The dark grey parts of the body are covered with grey spots; these spots are lighter on the pale grey parts of the body. Amid the pelagic populations, the young are not spotted; the spots only appear when the dolphins reach the age of sexual maturity.

Reproduction. The female's complete reproductive cycle lasts two to four years, depending on the population. The male reaches sexual maturity when it measures approximately 6 ft. (1.90 m), that is, between the ages of six and eight. For females, it is between the ages of four-and-a-half and eight-and-a-half and at a body length somewhere between 6 ft. 1 in. and 6 ft. 5 in. (1.87 and 1.95 m). Gestation lasts between 11 and 11½ months. Mating and births occur year-round. Lactation appears to last 11 months.

Population. The spotted dolphin is the species most affected by seine tuna fishing in the eastern tropical Pacific. During the early 1970s, more than 150,000 of these dolphins were caught each year by this

type of fishing. The number later fell to between 25,000 to 30,000 animals per year. The spotted dolphin is caught by the Japanese on the Izu peninsula and by the Solomon islanders. It is also caught in other types of fishing.

Diet. Unfortunately, in order to feed at the surface, this dolphin swims with schools of tuna; fisheries see it and take that as an indication of where to fish. It mostly feeds on epipelagic fish, such as flying fish, and both epipelagic and mesopelagic octopus.

Field identification. The spotted dolphin is very easily identified, as it jumps

acrobatically as it swims. It does not hesitate to go before ships and surfaces every
six to 10 seconds. It swims at a speed of 15
to 20 knots (27.7 to 37 km/hr) and can
reach a top speed of over 20 knots. This
dolphin does not jump so acrobatically
when it is not accompanying ships. It
moves in large herds about 100 strong, but
concentrations of 3,000 to 4,000 have also
been sighted.

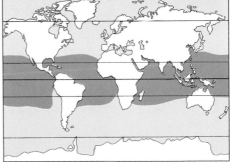

Communication—Sound emission.
The spotted dolphin has been recorded
emitting sound impulses of frequencies
up to 150 kHz and clicks of an unknown
frequency.

Distribution. It frequents the deep and
tropical waters of the Atlantic, Pacific, and
Indian oceans.

20. ATLANTIC SPOTTED DOLPHIN
Stenella plagiodon
(Cope, 1866)

Taxonomy.   In 1866 the American paleontologist E. D. Cope described the skull of a cetacean of unknown origin in his work on the history of the Delphinidae as *Delphinus plagiodon,* from the Greek *plagios,* oblique or inclined, and *odos (odontos),* a tooth. This dolphin was already known in 1817 under the name Bainville had given it: le dauphin de Pernetty, *Delphinus pernettensis.* Antoine Pernetty had described this dolphin, which he captured off the Brazilian coast in 1763 on an expedition led by L. A. de Bougainville.

Common names.   France: Dauphin de Pernetty. Great Britain: Atlantic spotted dolphin, Gulf Stream spotted dolphin, Spotter. Germany: Atlantischer fleckendelphin. Japan: Kasuri iruka.

Description.   The Atlantic spotted dolphin measures 6 ft. 6 in. (2 m) on an average and can reach 6 ft. 8 in. to 7 ft. 6 in. (2.20 to 2.30 m). It weighs between 240 and 265 lbs. (110 and 120 kg) and can reach 320 lbs. (145 kg). The newborn measures about 2 ft. 9 in. (90 cm). The adult's body, like the common dolphin's, is sturdy and fusiform. The snout is detached from the rest of the head. There are 34 to 37 small cone-shaped teeth on each side of both jaws. The dorsal fin is median, large, and falcate. The pectoral fins

are falcate and have pointed ends. The flukes have a median notch. The body's coloring varies with age. Young ones are light-colored and start getting the characteristic spots when they reach maturity. Adults are generally completely blue, and the back is darker than the stomach. There are white spots at the top of the flanks and

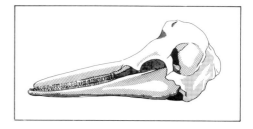

dark smudges towards the bottom and stomach. The fins are dark.

Reproduction.   Matings take place during the summer. The couple copulates vertically and both face each other. Gestation lasts 11 months and births occur mostly in June.

Population.   The Atlantic spotted dolphin is relatively common in the geographic area that it frequents, at least in the northwest Atlantic.

Diet.   This dolphin feeds on small fish, such as herring and anchovies, as well as on cephalopods, such as octopus.

Field identification.   The Atlantic spotted dolphin sometimes accompanies ships

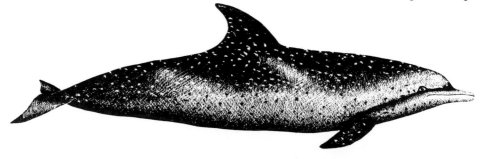

and sometimes stays away from them. It rarely jumps out of the water. When it emerges, the snout appears first, then the head, and finally the back, which is bent and shows the dorsal fin. It breathes three or four times a minute. When it ventilates quickly, it takes five quick breaths and immediately submerges for a minute or more. A specimen has been observed holding itself vertically, head down underwater, with its tail in the air. This behavior as well as the emersion sequence in which this dolphin's flukes never come out of the water remain unexplained. It generally swims at a speed of over 18 knots (33 km/hr). It is gregarious and moves in groups of 10 to 50, and sometimes even a few hundred. There have been reports of a solitary individual living off the coast of San Salvador in the Bahamas who appears to appreciate human company.

Communication—Sound emission.

This species emits clicks that are used for echolocation and in search of food. Pulse bursts, which are probably linked to an emotional context, have also been recorded. Each dolphin of this species

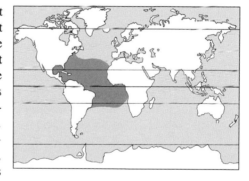

has its own whistle, called a signature whistle. Of the 1,580 whistles emitted by Atlantic spotted dolphins kept in two Florida aquariums (Marineland of Florida and Gulfarium), 97.3 percent are considered to have been signature whistles.

Distribution. This coastal species lives in the Atlantic, bordering the shores of the United States, South America, western Africa, and Europe, as well as the Gulf of Mexico and the Bahamas. It can be found up to 12.5 miles (20 km) from the shores and comes closer to them during the summer.

21. STRIPED DOLPHIN
Stenella coeruleolba
(Meyen, 1833)

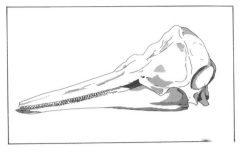

Taxonomy. The German zoologist F. J. Meyen described this dolphin in 1833 from a specimen captured off the east coast of South America. Its species name comes from its coloring: the Latin *caerelus,* blue-black, and *albus,* white. The striped dolphin comprises many geographic varieties; the following species have been classified under the species name *S. coeruleolba: S. styx* (Gray, 1846), *S. euphrosyne* (Peale, 1848), and *S. marginata* (Pucheran, 1868). It must also be noted that in 1971 Morzer Bruyns described a species living in the eastern part of the Mediterranean and bereft of black stripes: the Greek dolphin. All of the geographic variations are mostly differentiated by their coloring and size. (For example, the variation bordering the western Mediterranean is slightly smaller than that living off the western French coast in the Atlantic, and it appears that they form two separate populations.)

Common names. France: Dauphin de thétis. Great Britain: Striped dolphin, Streaker porpoise (fishermen), Euphrosyne dolphin. Germany: Blauweier delphin, Streifendelphin. Russia: Polosatyy del'fin. Latin America: Delfine listado. Japan: Suji iruka, Megane suji iruka.

Description. The striped dolphin measures 7 ft. 9 in. (2.40 m) on an average (6 ft. 6 in., or 2 m, for the Mediterranean species and 7 ft. 2 in., or 2.20 m, for the French Atlantic one). But it can reach 8 ft. 2 in. (2.50 m). Its average weight varies from 240 to 250 lbs. (110 to 115 kg), and it can reach a maximum of 310 lbs. (140 kg). Measurements of newborns, like those of adults, vary according to the different geographic populations, but they are in the range of 2 ft. 9 in. to 3 ft. 3 in. (90 cm to 1 m). The adult's body is slender and fusiform. The snout is distinct from the head and long and thin (but less pronounced than that of the common dolphin). There are 45 to 50 small cone-shaped teeth on each side of the upper jaw and 43 to 49 on each side of the lower. The dorsal fin is median, falcate, and medium-sized. The pectoral fins are short. The flukes show a pronounced notch. The back is dark grey to brown or a bluish grey, the flanks are lighter-colored, and the stomach is white. The eyes are circled in black. Two black stripes start from the eyes, one (which may be double) going to the anal area and the other (which may also be double) running to the pectorals. There is a dark falcate area under the dorsal fin, the point of which is directed towards the dolphin's front, with the base of this stain

remaining on the dark coloring of the back. The dorsal fin, the pectoral fins, the flukes, the upper jaw, and half the lower jaw are dark.

Reproduction. The female's complete reproductive cycle runs its course over two- and-a-half to three years. Males reach sexual maturity when they measure 7 ft. 2 in. (2.20 m), and females when they measure 6 ft. 8 in. (2.10 m), their average age at those lengths being nine years (or anywhere from five-and-a-half to 12½ years). Gestation is estimated at 12 months, and there seem to be two reproductive seasons for this species: fall and spring. Lactation lasts anywhere from eight to 18 months. Life expectancy is estimated at 50 years.

Population. The problems in connection with this dolphin and fisheries are particularly acute in Japan. Since before 1700, the striped dolphin has been caught by the Japanese for its flesh. In 1975, about 20,000 of these animals were driven towards a beach and harpooned. At that time, the Japanese estimated the local population at 400,000 to 600,000. The major Japanese ports for the capture of these animals are Kawana and Futo on the Izu peninsula and the island of Iki. These days the Japanese drive to the beach about 5,000 animals per year. In 1978 the population was estimated at 250,000 animals in the tropical east Pacific. At about 60 per year, the number of these dolphins that are caught there is certainly not alarming. In other parts of the world, the striped dolphin is often accidentally caught by fisheries. This species is quite common in the areas it frequents, except for the western Pacific. It has been noticed that in the western Mediterranean it has started occupying the biotope of the common dolphin, which appears to be disappearing from this region.

Diet. The striped dolphin feeds mostly on mesopelagic fish, or fish from depths of about 600 to 3,000 ft. In the Mediterranean, it feeds primarily on sardines and anchovies. It also consumes shrimp and octopus, but only in small quantities.

Field identification. The striped dolphin often jumps acrobatically out of the water. It surfaces every five seconds or every 10 to 20 seconds. It can jump about 20 ft. (6 to 7 m) high and sometimes lands on its side. Ships attract herds of these dolphins, which come and play in their bow waves. They stay there an unpredictable amount of time and then leave abruptly without anyone knowing why. This species swims at a top speed of 15 to 17 knots (27.7 to 31.1 km/hr), but it can go up to 20 knots (37 km/hr). This is a highly gregarious dolphin that swims in bands of 10 to 20 individuals, or sometimes groups of many hundreds. In the tropical eastern Pacific, striped dolphins sometimes swim with schools of albacore tuna *(Thunnus albacares)*.

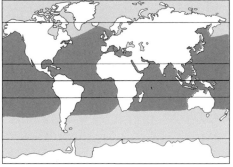

Communication—Sound emission. We have no data on this topic for this animal at present.

Distribution. The striped dolphin is found in temperate, tropical, and subtropical waters around the world. It prefers deep water and remains rare in coastal areas. It carries out a local migration around the equator in the fall, travelling towards higher latitudes in the spring.

22. SPINNER DOLPHIN
Stenella longirostris
(Gray, 1828)

Taxonomy.   The skull of a dolphin of unknown origin was briefly described by the British naturalist Gray in 1828 under the name *Delphinus longirostris,* from the Latin *longis,* long, and *rostrum,* beak. There are five geographic varieties as well as a dwarfish variety, but currently only one species is recognized.

Common names.   Great Britain: Spinner dolphin, Long-snouted dolphin. Latin America: Delfin tornillon, Delfin churumbelo. Russia: Dlinnonosyy, Vertyasshchiysya del'fin. Germany: Spinnerdelphin. Japan: Hashi naga iruka.

Description.   The five geographic varieties and the dwarfish variety:

• The Costa Rican Form.   This type measures between 5 ft. 10 in. and 6 ft. 6 in. (1.80 and 2.20 m) and weighs approximately 150 lbs. (68 kg). The body is long and thin, and the snout is rather long. The dorsal fin is triangular and leans towards the front in older animals. The pectoral fins are small and thin. The body is dark grey on the back and light grey on the stomach. This dolphin lives along the Pacific coasts of Central America (notably, Nicaragua, Costa Rica, and Panama). It has about 100 small cone-shaped teeth on each jaw.

• The Eastern Pacific Form.   It measures between 5 ft. 2 in. and 6 ft. 2 in. (1.60 and 1.90 m) and weighs 130 lbs. (60 kg) on an average. The body is short and slender, and the snout is quite short in comparison with the preceding type. There is a bulge on the ventral side between the tail and anal areas. In older individuals, there are dorsal and ventral careens on the peduncle caudal. This geographic type also has 100 small cone-shaped teeth on each jaw. Its back is a dark grey that lightens on the flanks and ends in white on the stomach. It frequents the coasts of the tropical Pacific Ocean of North America, from Tres Marias Islands to Acapulco. It can be found as far as 625 miles (1,000 km) from the shore (some reports say 1,200 miles, or 1,900 km).

• The White-Belly Form.   The adult measures between 5 ft. 2 in. and 6 ft. 2 in. (1.60 and 1.90 m) and weighs 132 lbs. (60 kg) on an average. The body is short and stocky. The dorsal fin is triangular or falcate. There is a bulge, or protuberance, on the ventral side of the caudal peduncle. The pectorals are small and thin. The snout is relatively long. The back is a dark grey, which is clearly demarcated from the pure white of the ventral region and flanks. The upper jaw is black. This type is found off the coasts of Mexico, Central America, and the northern portion of South America (185 to 500 miles, or 300 to 800 km, from the shore).

• The Tropical Atlantic Ocean and Indian Ocean Form.   This dolphin measures 5 ft. 10 in. (1.80 m) but can reach 6 ft. 6 in. (2 m), and its weight is estimated

Hawaiian variety

Costa Rican variety

at 180 lbs. (82 kg). The snout's length varies from one endemic population to the next. The dorsal fin is falcate, and the peduncles are medium-sized. The back is dark grey, with lighter flanks and a white stomach. The tip of the snout and the lips are black. There are between 92 and 130 small cone-shaped teeth on each jaw. It is found in the Atlantic's tropical waters, the Gulf of Mexico,and the tropical Indian Ocean.

• The Hawaiian Form. The adult measures between 5 ft. 6 in. and 6 ft. 6 in. (1.70 and 2 m) and weighs 200 lbs. (90 kg). Its body is fusiform, and it has a long, thin snout. The dorsal fin is falcate, and the flippers are of a medium size. This type's coloring is more pronounced than that of the other four. It has a dark grey area starting at the tip of the melon and extending all the way to the back of the dorsal fin. A lighter grey band starts at the bottom of the melon and runs along the flanks to the base of the caudal fin; it rejoins at the anal region and colors the entire peduncle. The stomach is white from the snout to the anus. The upper jaw, the tip of the lower jaw, and the fins are dark grey. The eyes are rimmed in black. This type lives in the Hawaiian waters, but it

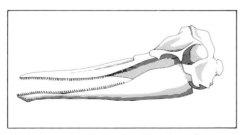

has been recorded as having been seen to the east, off San Diego.

• The Dwarfish Form. This type is known only from 10 skeletons held in the Tokyo National Science Museum. We can only comment on its originality. It differs

from the other types by its body size of 4 ft. to 4 ft. 6 in. (1.29 to 1.37 m), the size of its skull, and the average number of its vertebrae. Adults apparently weigh between 48 and 58 lbs. (21.5 and 26.5 kg). It is only found in the Gulf of Siam; its population size and status are completely unknown.

Reproduction. We have very little data on this long-snouted dolphin's reproduction. The male of the eastern Pacific type reaches sexual maturity when it measures an average of 5 ft. 6 in. (1.70 m), which usually occurs between the ages of six and 11½ years. For the female, it is when she reaches 5 ft. 4 in. (1.65 m), usually between the ages of three years, seven months and five years. Gestation lasts 10 months and six days, and the newborn measures an average of 2 ft. 5 in. (77 cm). The female's complete reproductive cycle lasts two years.

Population. This is the dolphin species that is most affected by seine-tuna-fishing operations. During the early 1970s, the number of dolphins caught in nets was enormous, more than 35,000 a year: 41,000 in 1970, 38,000 in 1971, and 42,000 in 1972. Currently, about 7,000 to 10,000 animals are caught each year. In 1978 the total spinner dolphin population (eastern Pacific and white-belly types) in the fishing areas was estimated at 2,000,000 animals, and it is probable that these captures have seriously damaged this species' population. It is estimated that its population has declined as much as 80 percent since seine fishing started in the 1960s. In the Solomon Islands, New Guinea, and Japan, these animals are driven to shore; in the Caribbean, they are harpooned.

Diet. This long-snouted dolphin feeds on mesopelagic fish as well as on epipelagic

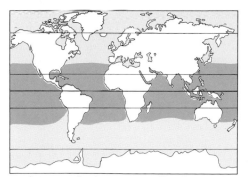

can travel at a top speed of 20 knots (37 km/hr). This dolphin is very gregarious and moves in bands of three to many hundreds. It is believed that it can dive to a depth of 200 ft. (60 m) to feed itself. It has often been seen swimming in the company of spotted dolphins in the eastern Pacific and with humpback whales near Hawaii. It has been the victim of some mass strandings in Florida (36 individuals in 1961 and 28 in 1976).

and mesopelagic octopus. It often swims with the spotted dolphin, but its feeding area goes much deeper.

Field identification. This dolphin breathes many times per minute. It does not fear boats and often accompanies them for half an hour or more to play by their stem. It performs impressive jumps, and it is said to be able to rotate seven times on a longitudinal axis during a single jump. The spinner dolphin is a speedy swimmer that

Communication—Sound emission.
This species has a large repertoire of sounds such as clicks, high-pitched cries, and pulse bursts.

Distribution. The spinner dolphin is a species that lives in deep waters and is found in the hot tropical waters of the Atlantic, Pacific, and Indian oceans. For the geographic distribution of each type, refer back to the type descriptions.

23. CLYMENE DOLPHIN
Stenella clymene
(Gray, 1850)

Taxonomy. The British naturalist Gray described this dolphin from a cetacean skull of unknown origin in 1850. The skull resembled that of the long-snouted spinner dolphin in its general architecture, but it had few teeth. The name is from the Greek *klymenos,* for famous or first-rate, or after Clymene, a daughter of Tethys, the Titan Japet's wife, and the mother of Atlas, Phaeton, and Heliades. It was thought to be a geographic variation of *Stenella lon-girostris* until 1976, when an individual landed on the New Jersey coast. A few months later, it was decided to classify this dolphin as a separate species.

Common names. Great Britain: Helmet dolphin, Short-snouted spinner dolphin.

Description. This dolphin measures an average of 5 ft. 10 in. (1.80 m) and can reach 6 ft. 6 in. (2 m). It weighs between 165 and 200 lbs. (75 and 90 kg). The new-born is believed to measure 2 ft. 5 in. (77 cm). The adult's body is fusiform. The snout is shorter than in the long-snouted dolphin; the pectoral and dorsal fins are 10 percent smaller. The adult's coloring is almost identical to that of the Hawaiian type *Stenella longirostris.* There is a long black cape, starting at the melon and running down to half of the caudal peduncle, which spills over a little onto the flanks. A grey

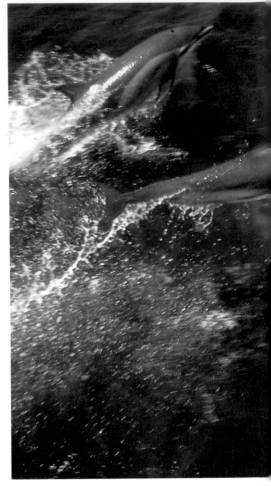

stripe extends from the snout, going by the eyes and rejoining the caudal peduncle. The lower jaw (except its tip), throat, and stomach down to the anal region are white. The tip of the snout, the lips, and the pec-toral, caudal, and dorsal fins are black. The eyes are circled in black. There are 38

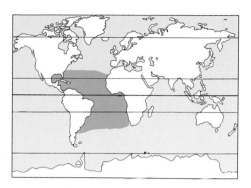

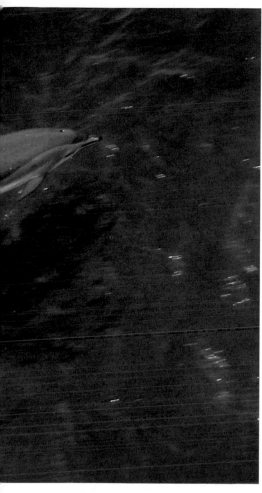

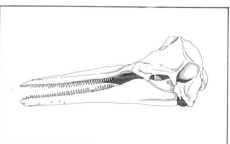

Population. The clymene dolphin is presumed rare, but we do not have any data on its population since it is a new species for science.

Diet. This dolphin's diet is probably composed of small mesopelagic fish and particularly of Myctophidae (lantern fish), which it eats at half-depth during the day, or at night when these fish come to the surface.

Field identification. Most observations of this dolphin have been carried out at some depth (which is justified by its basic diet). It spins and jumps spectacularly but is still less acrobatic than the long-snouted dolphin. It has been reported that, in the Gulf of Guinea and off eastern Africa, this dolphin plays with the bow waves of ships. It is gregarious and appears to move in small groups.

Communication—Sound emission.
There is no data on this topic for this species.

to 49 pointed teeth on each side of the two jaws.

Reproduction. Since this dolphin has only been considered an irrefutable species for a short time, we have no information on its reproductive habits.

Distribution. The clymene dolphin only lives in the warm tropical and subtropical waters of the Atlantic. In the west, its habitat extends from New Jersey to the Caribbean, and in the east, to the coasts of northwestern Africa.

24. BOTTLENOSE DOLPHIN
Tursiops truncatus
(Montagu, 1821)

Taxonomy. Although this dolphin had long been known and was even studied by the French naturalist B. Lacépède before its definitive description, it was the Englishman G. Montagu who described it in 1821, from a specimen that had run aground in 1814, under the name *Delphinus truncatus,* from the Latin *truncare,* cut. Later the genus name *Tursiops* was added, from the Latin *tursio,* an animal that resembles a dolphin, and *ops,* head. Many species have been described, but currently only one species and its three geographic types are recognized. The three distinct subspecies are *T.t. truncatus* (Montagu, 1821) from the Atlantic Ocean, *T.t. gilli* (Dall, 1873) from the Pacific Ocean, and *T.t. aduncus* (Ehrenberg, 1832) from the tropical Indian Ocean.

Common names. France: Souffleur, Dauphin à gros nez, Dauphin tronqué. Great Britain: Bottlenose dolphin. Germany: Groertümmler. Russia: Bolshoi delfin. Latin America: Delfin nariz de botella. Japan: Bando iruka.

Description. The male bottlenose dolphin measures 10 ft. (3 m) on an average and can reach 13 ft. (4 m). Its average weight is 440 lbs. (200 kg), and it can reach 1,430 lbs. (650 kg). The newborn measures between 2 ft. 9 in. and 4 ft. 3 in. (90 cm and 1.30 m) and weighs about 66 lbs. (30 kg). The bottlenose dolphin's body is slender and robust. The melon is quite convex; the snout is well defined, short, and wide; and the lower jaw is longer than the upper. The dorsal fin is

median, high, and falcate. The pectoral fins are relatively short and falcate. The flukes have a somewhat pronounced median notch. There are 18 to 26 small cone-shaped teeth on each side of both jaws. The dolphin's back is a medium or dark grey, while its flanks are light grey and its stomach white or pink.

Reproduction. The female gives birth every two to three years. It becomes sexually mature between the ages of five and 12, whereas, for males, it is between the ages of 10 and 12. Gestation lasts a year, and births occur in the spring (February to

May)—and probably in the fall (September to November) off the coast of Florida. In European waters, births take place in midsummer. Lactation lasts 12 to 18 months. Life expectancy is estimated at 35 years or more. In captivity, this animal has given birth to hybrids with Risso's dolphin, pilot whales, false killer whales, and the rough-toothed dolphin, but the only

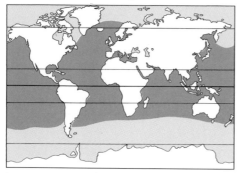

known cases of hybridization in nature have been with Risso's dolphin.

Population. There is no estimate of the total global bottlenose dolphin population. It is regarded as a common cetacean, and it is too large and strong to be captured by accident. However, it is fished in many places, especially off the eastern United States and in the Black Sea, but only to excess in Japan. This is the species usually found in aquariums. It is also well known, due to the TV series ''Flipper.''

Diet. For this dolphin, food varies with location. Mullets, catfish, eels, rays, shrimp, crabs, octopus, and even small sharks are in its diet. In captivity, the bottlenose dolphin consumes between 13 and 33 lbs. (6 and 15 kg) of food per day.

Field identification. The bottlenose dolphin is a rather friendly animal, as those who have visited aquariums have had the pleasure of discovering. It surfaces two or three times per minute while swimming and stays immersed for periods of seven to 10 minutes. Its cruising speed is 5 to 6 knots (9.2 to 11 km/hr), sometimes 13 to 18 knots (24 to 33.3 km/hr), and it can go above a speed of 20 knots (37 km/hr). This dolphin occasionally plays in ships' bow waves, but it remains cautious around motor boats. There have been cases in which solitary individuals have come near the coastline and attempted to make contact with people (France, Great Britain). This is a gregarious cetacean, travelling in herds of hundreds of animals split into small groups of about 12. Herds comprising more than 40 animals have been sighted off Florida. The bottlenose dolphin has been seen travelling with bands of Risso's dolphins and long-finned pilot whales.

Communication—Sound emission. This species emits high-frequency echolocation signals ranging from 4 to 170 kHz. Some of these clicks sound like a creaking door and then turn into a whistle. The clicks are emitted between 30 and 800 times per second. It has been demonstrated that this dolphin can only hear sounds at a frequency of up to 150 kHz.

Distribution. This dolphin has a worldwide distribution, from temperate to tropical waters. It is usually a coastal animal, but it can also be found very far out at sea.

25. RISSO'S DOLPHIN
Grampus griseus
(Cuvier, 1812)

Taxonomy. The French scientist G. Cuvier described this species under the name *Delphinus griseus,* from the Latin *griseus,* grey, from a drawing and description by an amateur naturalist named M. Risso, who had based his observations on a dolphin that had run aground near Nice (France). Another had run aground at the beginning of the century in Brest, Brittany (France), but only its skull and a skin sample had been saved for scientific purposes. In 1828 the British naturalist Gray created a new genus called *Grampus* for this animal, from the Latin *grandis,* big, and *piscis,* fish.

Common names. France: Dauphin gris, Grampus. Great Britain: Risso's dolphin, Grampus, White-headed grampus. Latin America: Delfin de Risso, Falson caldern, Delfin gris. Russia: Seryy del'fin. Germany: Rundkopfdelphin, Rissodelphin. Japan: Hanna gondo kujira.

Description. Risso's dolphin measures an average of 10 ft. (3 m), with a maximum of 14 ft. 1 in. (4.30 m). Its average weight is 660 lbs. (300 kg), but it can reach as much as 1,500 lbs. (680 kg). The newborn measures from 4 ft. 6 in. to 5 ft. 10 in. (1.40 to 1.80 m). The body is generally sturdy, and the part behind the dorsal fin is slender. The melon is huge and divided by a slight vertical linear depression running from the forehead to the mouth. The snout is almost nonexistent. The dorsal fin is median, falcate, predominant, and high (about 16 in., or 40 cm). The pectoral and caudal fins are long in comparison to those of other cetaceans, and the tail has a median notch. There are only one or two vestigial teeth on the upper jaw and three to seven large cone-shaped teeth on each side of the lower jaw. The adult's body is dark grey, with a long white area on the throat, chest, and stomach. The fins are black. Young animals have a yellowish head and are generally lighter-colored than adults. As these cetaceans age, they are covered with linear scars that result from tooth marks left by their fellow mammals or cephalopods; some are so covered with these gashes that they are almost completely white.

Reproduction. It is believed that the female of this species becomes sexually mature when it reaches a length of approximately 9 ft. (2.70 m). For males, it is between 8 ft. 6 in. and 10 ft. (2.60 and 3 m). Gestation is thought to last a year, and births occur mostly during the winter (between December and April) in warm wa-

ters. A summer birth has been reported in the Mediterranean. Life expectancy is estimated at a minimum of 20 years. However, based on observations of an animal known as Pelorus Jack in New Zealand that lived close to 24 years, it is possible that this animal can live up to 30 or more years.

Population. We have no estimates of its total population, but Risso's dolphin seems to be common in warm and temperate waters. Some are captured by small cetacean fisheries in Japan (between 1976 and 1981, 723 were reportedly captured), the Caribbean, Newfoundland (Canada), and Indonesia. There are some accidental catches in the northeast Atlantic (France) and in the western Mediterranean (11 caught in four years), off the Japanese coast (75 captured between 1976 and 1981 in set nets), and in tuna nets in the east central Pacific (it is estimated that as many as 7,500 are affected by this activity).

Diet. Due to its dentition, Risso's dolphin feeds mostly on cephalopods and occasionally on fish.

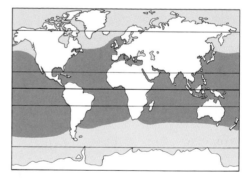

Field identification. Risso's dolphin surfaces to breathe almost every six seconds, but it is also reported that it ventilates its lungs every 15 to 20 seconds during a three to four minute period. It then dives and remains submerged for one or two minutes, and it can make its apnea last for up to half an hour. Sometimes it surfaces, showing its melon, back, and dorsal fin, and then disappears; when in a group, it often jumps acrobatically. The breath is detectable. It is said that this is a timid animal, and while it is true that it rarely approaches ships, stories are often heard of some of these animals playing in the waves made by slow ships. Risso's dolphin is a spectacular jumper, which is rare for such a massive animal. It can swim at a high speed of up to 15 knots (27.7 km/hr) and can hold a top speed of 17 knots (31. km/hr) for five minutes. It practises "spy hopping" by holding itself vertically in the water, with its head and flippers above water level. It swims with spinner dolphins, northern right whale dolphins, long- and short-finned pilot whales, and bottlenose dolphins, which helps to explain the stranding of three *Grampius X tursiops* hybrids in May, 1933, on Ireland's western coast and the 13 cases of hybridization in captivity at Marineland in Enoshima, Japan. This cetacean is gregarious, swimming alone, in couples, or in groups of five or more in areas where it is abundant.

Communication—Sound emission.
We have no data on this topic at the present time for this species.

Distribution. Risso's dolphin is found all over, but mostly in deep temperate and tropical waters (60 to 80 °F, or 15 to 25 °C). There are probably some seasonal migrations in the North Atlantic: It goes north in the summer and south in the winter.

26. SOUTHERN RIGHT WHALE DOLPHIN
Lissodelphis peronii
(Lacépède, 1804)

Taxonomy. The French naturalist F. Peron observed this species while on an expedition to Australia from 1800 to 1804 aboard the ship *Le Géographe*. Upon his return to Paris, he gave the description to B. Lacépède, who published it in his treatise on natural history in 1804. In 1841, the German C. Cloger proposed a genus name for this somewhat special cetacean, from the Greek *lisso,* smooth, and *delphis,* dolphin, and in honor of the French naturalist who first described it.

Common names. France: Dauphin de Peron, Lissodelphis de Peron. Great Britain: Southern right whale dolphin. Spain: Delfinliso. Latin America: Tunina sin aleta, Delfin liso. Germany: Südlicher glattdelphin. Japan: Shiro hara semi iruka.

Description. The southern right whale dolphin measures 5 ft. 10 in. (1.80 m) on an average and can reach a maximum of 7 ft. 9 in. (2.40 m). Its average weight varies from 130 to 140 lbs. (60 to 65 kg), and it can reach a maximum of 180 lbs. (82 kg). The adult's body is slender, hydrodynamic, and without a dorsal fin. The pectoral and caudal fins are small in proportion to the rest of the animal's body.

The tail has a median notch. There are 43 to 47 small pointed teeth on each side of both jaws. Its back is black from the back of the snout demarcation to the tail. This coloring spills over onto the flanks and spreads to the base of the pectorals. The snout, the entire ventral area (including

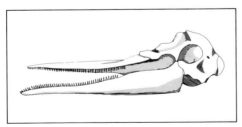

the tail, except for its edges), and the pectoral fins are white.

Reproduction. At present, we have no data on the southern right whale dolphin's reproduction.

Population. We lack an estimate of the southern right whale's total population.

This dolphin is said to be rare, but it seems to be common at lower latitudes. Specimens were captured by whalers during the nineteenth century, and some still are today by Chilean fishermen.

Diet. This cetacean eats lantern fish (Myctophidae) and octopus.

Field identification. When this dolphin swims slowly, its back alone emerges above the water's surface, which makes it very unobtrusive. As soon as a ship is in the area, it swims faster and groups get into formations that jump acrobatically at great speed and in perfect synchronization. A fast swimmer, this dolphin can reach a top speed of 15 knots (27 km/hr). The number of individuals in the groups observed to date varies greatly; it can be anywhere from two to 500. According to Watson, the number of individuals varies from 30 to 100. A herd of more than 1,000 was observed off New Zealand in 1964 and in the south Indian Ocean in 1968. This dolphin sometimes swims with dusky dolphins, Pacific white-beaked dolphins, and pilot whales. The southern right whale dolphin has had a few mass strandings in New Zealand.

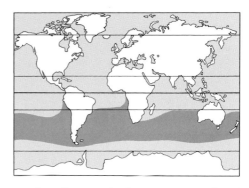

Communication—Sound emission.
We currently have no data on this topic for this species.

Distribution. This is a pelagic species and frequents the temperate and subantarctic waters of the Pacific Ocean, the Tasmanian Sea, and the waters south of Australia. In Chile, this species is found between Latitude 19° S and Cape Horn.

27. NORTHERN RIGHT WHALE DOLPHIN
Lissodelphis borealis
(Peale, 1848)

Taxonomy. Up until 1848, when the American painter T. Peale captured a specimen in the Pacific Northwest, this strange dolphin was only known by whalers and had no scientific name. Peale called it *Delphinapterus borealis,* which means northern wingless dolphin. Years later, the genus name created by the German zoologist C. Cloger was given to the species.

Common names. France: Dauphin à dos lisse boréal. Great Britain: Northern right whale dolphin. Latin America: Delfin de liso. Russia: Severnyy kitovidnyy del'fin. Germany: Nördlicher glattdelphin. Japan: Semi iruka, Kiti demi iruka.

Description. The northern right whale dolphin measures 6 ft. 6 in. (2 m) on an average; the largest known male measured 12 ft. (3.70 m) and the largest female 7 ft. 6 in. (2.30 m). Its average weight is 155 lbs. (70 kg), and it can reach a maximum of 175 to 200 lbs. (80 to 90 kg). Newborns measure 1 ft. 9 in. to 2 ft. 3 in. (60 to 70

cm). The adult's body is hydrodynamic and slender, and it lacks a dorsal fin. The pectoral fins as well as the caudal one are small when compared to the rest of the body. The tail has a median notch. There are 37 to 43 small pointed teeth on each side of the upper jaw and 40 to 46 on each side of the lower jaw. The young are pale grey to brown on their back and flanks. Adults have a black back and black flanks to the level of the belly button. The caudal and pectoral fins are black above and white below. There is a white spot by the lower jaw. Individuals appear to vary in their coloring.

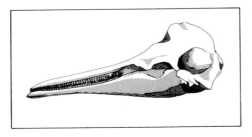

Reproduction. Males are sexually mature when they measure about 6 ft. 9 in. (2.10 m); for females, it is when they reach about 6 ft. 5 in. (1.98 m). Births take place in April and May.

Population. This cetacean is relatively common in the regions it inhabits. However, we have no estimate of its total population. It is captured, both intentionally and by accident. It is harpooned by the tuna and whiting fishermen of Japan, mostly between the prefectures of Aomori and Ibaragi, or caught in seine nets.

Diet. This species feeds primarily on mesopelagic fish; mostly lantern fish (Myctophidae) have been found in its stomach, but also Bathylagidae, *Melamphaidae paralepididae,* and some *Cololabis saira.*

Field identification. Watson reported that, when this animal is not disturbed, it swims slowly, breathing every 20 to 30 seconds. It is then hard to see and locate and can be taken for a school of fish. But when disturbed, it becomes furious and starts making low jumps. It is a fast swimmer, going at a speed of 15 to 17 knots (27.7 to 31 km/hr) or even faster. When it jumps, it arches its body above the water. When it is being chased, it can disappear underwater for six minutes or more. It is very gregarious, swimming in groups of 30 to 40, either in a "V" formation or side by side. It can be part of a herd of many hundreds (up to 2,000). It often swims with short-finned pilot whales, Pacific white-sided dolphins, common dolphins,

Risso's dolphins, Dall's porpoises, northern rorquals, humpback whales, and even California seals.

Communication—Sound emission.
This cetacean has been the object of many acoustic studies in its natural habitat. For echolocation, it emits a rapid series of clicks of a frequency above 40 kHz. It also emits impulsive sounds, whistles, whimpers, and yelps.

Distribution. This species is only found in the cold and temperate waters of the North Pacific, rarely going into waters warmer than 65 °F (19 °C), from Japan to the Sea of Okhotsk in the west and from

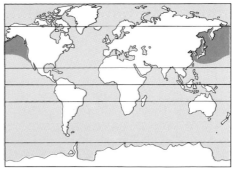

Alaska to Baja California in the east. It lives in the open sea in deep water. It carries out a sort of migration, frequenting the waters of southern California from October or November to April. The west Pacific populations go south in the fall or winter.

28. HECTOR'S DOLPHIN
Cephalorhynchus hectori
(Van Beneden, 1881)

Taxonomy. J. Hector, curator of the Wellington Colonial Museum in New Zealand, described a dolphin of this species in 1873. He then sent a specimen to the Belgian paleontologist Van Beneden, who identified the animal as a completely new cetacean. In 1885 Hector put the dolphin into the appropriate taxonomic classification—from the Greek *kephalos,* head, and *rhynghos,* nose, and *hectori,* in reference to himself.

Common names. France: Dauphin d'Hector, Céphalorhynque à front blanc, Dauphin de Nouvelle-Zélande. Great Britain: Hector's dolphin, New Zealand dolphin. Germany: Hectordelphin, Neuseeland-delphin. Japan: Seppari iruka, Kaoshiro iruka.

Description. Females of this species measure a maximum of about 4 ft. 8 in. (1.44 m), and males about 4 ft. 3 in. (1.32 m). The maximum weight hovers around 105 lbs. (48 kg) for females and 83 lbs. (38 kg) for males. The newborn measures 2 ft. 5 in. (76 cm) and weighs 17 to 22 lbs. (8 to 10 kg). The dolphin's body is stocky with a slightly rounded snout that is hard to distinguish. There are 30 to 32 small cone-shaped teeth on each side of both jaws. The dorsal fin is median, rounded, and low. The pectoral fins are paddle-shaped. The flukes have a median notch. Hector's dolphin is generally dark grey on the dorsal area and flanks, whereas the tips of the jaws, the bottom of the upper jaw, and all the way to the pectoral fins, as well as the dorsal and caudal fins, are darker, almost black. It has a sort of pale grey, sometimes white, bonnet on its forehead, from the front of the blowhole to right above the eyes. This lighter coloring sometimes extends to the tip of the upper jaw in older animals. The stomach area is white from the chin to the anal region. Most individuals have a dark spot around the anus. Newborns are a darker grey, with a yellowish tinge. As of birth, there is a series of four to six pale vertical bands on each side of the body from the pectoral fins to the anus; these are very obvious at three months and disappear completely after six months.

Reproduction. Data concerning the reproductive biology of Hector's dolphin is

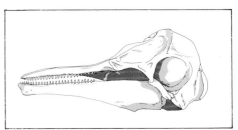

recent and comes from New Zealand. These dolphins are sexually mature at the age of seven; the minimum measurements for sexual maturity in the female are 4 ft. 6 in. (1.39 m) at 98 lbs. (44 kg), and 3 ft. 8 in. (1.17 m) at 68 lbs. (31 kg) for the male. Mating mostly takes place during the austral summer and fall. We still do not know how long gestation lasts. Births

take place during the austral spring and early summer (November to February). Females give birth to a single offspring every two to three years. It is believed that the female only has three to five babies in her lifetime. Lactation lasts at least a year, and the baby begins feeding on solid foods at six months. The life expectancy for this species is estimated at 18 years.

Population. Hector's dolphin is endemic to New Zealand. We do not know whether the population is stable or in decline. On an average, 11 animals are accidentally caught each year, by drift net or trawl. On the north shore of Banks Peninsula, 44 dolphins were caught by a single fisherman during the 1985–86 season. The average number of catches per year in this region is 50 to 90 (the total population in Banks Peninsula is estimated at 650 to 700). Since this species inhabits a specific area, has a low level of reproduction, and is often accidentally caught in nets, it is considered endangered.

Diet. Hector's dolphin feeds mostly on pelagic and benthic species living below the violent weather zone. Remains of *Tracharus novaezelandis, Physoculus bachus, Crepalatus novaezelandiae,* as well as Engraulidae otolithes (anchovies) have been found in their stomach. The stomach of two individuals also contained shells, octopus, and crustaceans.

Field identification. Hector's dolphin jumps out of the water to impress a prospective mate or in other interactions. When it surfaces to breathe, only its dorsal fin is apparent. It quickly jumps through the water, showing only small parts of its body at a time. Normally, it breathes two or four times every 10 to 50 seconds, between dives of one to two minutes. When feeding, it remains submerged 90 seconds. It rarely goes above 2 or 3 knots (3.7 to 5.5 km/hr), but its top speed could be in the vicinity of 6 to 8 knots (11 to 13 km/hr). This dolphin accompanies fishing boats to ports and tries to approach large ships. It is not shy and is often seen near-

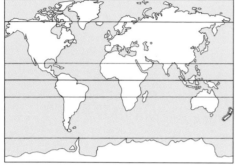

ing New Zealand's beaches to play with the swimmers, particularly children. It usually moves in groups of three to 10, but some groups of up to 300 have been seen off river bars (of the Rakaia and Kawhia rivers). Four animals are being kept in captivity at Napier Marineland in New Zealand, but they are not adapting well.

Communication—Sound emission.
Hector's dolphin is a "talkative" cetacean in its natural habitat and does not hesitate to come near hydrophones; it emits high-frequency sounds of about 120 kHz. As with the Commerson's dolphin, it has two types of sound pulse: single pulses under 200 s and double pulses under 400 s, with repetition rates of 1 to 600 Hz.

Distribution. Hector's dolphin is a coastal species (living less than 5 miles, or 8 km, from the shore). It is very common in the waters off the central and eastern parts of New Zealand, but it is also found in those off Australia and probably Sarawak and Borneo. It is said to frequent muddy waters and not to mind travelling to the estuaries of the Clarence, Gray, and Wangavi rivers in New Zealand. This dolphin carries out a small-scale migration around New Zealand, emigrating towards the North Island in December and January and returning to the South Island in February.

29. HEAVISIDE'S DOLPHIN
Cephalorhynchus heavisidii
(Gray, 1828)

Taxonomy. In 1827 Captain Heaviside, an employee of the British East India Company, sent a skull and swatch of skin from a dolphin of this species from the Cape of Good Hope back to London. In 1828 the British naturalist Gray identified this cetacean by the scientific name *Delphinus heavisidii*.

Common names. France: Dauphin de Heaviside, Céphalorhynque du Cap. Great Britain: Heaviside's dolphin. Germany: Heaviside delphin, Kapdelphin. Japan: Kosyachi iruka.

Description. Heaviside's dolphin measures 4 ft. 9 in. (1.50 m) on an average and can reach 5 ft. 6 in. (1.70 m). Its average weight varies from 90 to 110 lbs. (40 to 50 kg), and it can reach a maximum of 155 lbs. (70 kg). The adult's body is stocky, with a cone-shaped head; the melon is rounded and the snout is not distinct. There are 25 to 30 small, pointed teeth on each side of both jaws. The dorsal fin is low, triangular, and median. The pectorals are small and black, measuring 12 to 18 percent of the animal's body length. Their lower edge is serrated in the adult. The caudal fin has a median notch. This dolphin is generally blue-black dorsally, with a grey cape on the head and thoracic region. The stomach has a grey flame with four well-defined uncolored ar-

eas: a sort of white collar between the pectorals and a white stain divided into three branches starting at the level of the pectoral fins and extending to the anal region. The fins are black, except for the ventral face of the pectorals, which is white. Some totally albino animals have been observed and photographed.

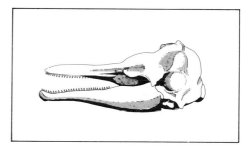

Reproduction. We have little data on this animal's reproduction. It measures about 2 ft. 6 in. (80 cm) at birth. The smallest specimen ever observed was a male that ran aground in January 1986. Probably a newborn, it was 2 ft. 8 in., or 84.7 cm, long and weighed 21 lbs., or 9.5 kg.

Population. We know little about the Heaviside dolphin population, but we do know that this species is considered rare. A few specimens are probably accidentally captured by anchovy fisheries, and two were reportedly captured by a Portuguese trawler. Less than 100 are reportedly caught each year by the seine nets off South Africa's western coasts, up to Namibia. Bullets have been found in the bodies of some stranded animals, leading

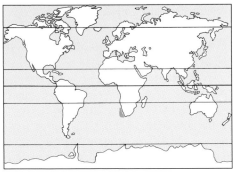

Field identification. Few observations of this species have been carried out. It has been spotted swimming both slowly and fast, sometimes jumping out of the water. It does not appear to be shy and is seen accompanying small ships and fishing boats, playing for hours before their stems, which helps to explain its vulnerability to accidental catches by fishermen.

us to believe that there is some sort of contact between these dolphins and fishermen. (This contact may be rather common off the Namibian coast.)

Communication—Sound emission. In 1969 sound impulses of up to 8 kHz were observed in this species.

Diet. The Heaviside dolphin probably feeds on octopus and fish living at the bottom of the sea.

Distribution. Heaviside's dolphin lives in the coastal waters off southern Africa (up to five nautical miles from the shore), from the Cape of Good Hope to Cape Cross in Namibia.

30. CHILEAN DOLPHIN
Cephalorhynchus Eutropia
(Gray, 1846)

Taxonomy. The first-known individual of this species was drawn by the British naturalist Gray in 1846, without any accompanying commentary, from a specimen collected off the southern coast of Chile. It was not until 1893 that more specimens were obtained and this dolphin became better known. The name *eutropia* comes from the Greek *eu,* good or true, and *tropidos,* keel or careen, in reference to the shape of its skull.

Common names. Great Britain: Chilean dolphin, Black dolphin. Latin America: Delfin negro, Tunina negra, Delfin chileno. Japan: Harajiro iruka.

Description. The male of this species measures 4 ft. 8 in. to 5 ft. 6 in. (1.47 to 1.67 m), and the females measure 4 ft. 5 in. to 5 ft. 4 in. (1.36 to 1.65 m). It weighs between 100 and 130 lbs. (45 and 60 kg) and has a small and sturdy body, with a short, round face and an only slightly distinct snout. There are 28 to 31 cone-shaped teeth on each side of both jaws. The dorsal fin is very low, triangular, and median, with a longer attack margin and a blunter, or duller, apex. The pectoral fins are small and the caudal has a median notch. There is a careen above and beyond the caudal peduncle. The back and flanks are black, as are the pectoral, dorsal, and caudal fins. There are four white areas on the ventral

side: one under the throat, one behind each pectoral fin, and one around the anal region. The blowhole's perimeter is sometimes pale grey. The lips have a thin pale grey or white margin.

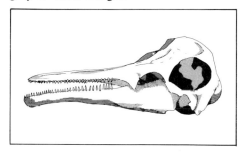

Diet. We know little about this animal's diet. It eats octopus *(Loligo gahi)* and crustaceans *(Munida Subrugosa),* and it sometimes plays with salmon, which it must also feed on.

Reproduction. We have no data on this animal's reproduction. Young have been seen in groups in October, January, March, and April near Valdivia and in December at Isla Chiloé.

Population. This dolphin is considered to be very rare. Some are accidentally caught in drift nets off the Chilean coast and then used as crab bait, which will probably affect their numbers. We cannot estimate the total population or the number of individuals captured each year.

Field identification. Unfortunately, very few reports exist on this species in its natural habitat. It is thought to be a slow swim-

mer, with a probable maximum speed of 6 to 8 knots (11 to 15 km/hr). It undulates through the water, as do sea lions, probably breathing every five to 10 seconds. It occasionally jumps out of the water, diving back in headfirst or falling in on its side. It seems rather shy towards ships and moves alone or in small groups of six to 12. One herd of 30 was seen in the Strait of Magellan. Out at sea, close to the southern limit of its habitat, it is said to swim in large groups of 20 to 400 (this last figure could include the total number of individuals in many small groups). These dolphins have been seen in the company of Peale's dolphins and once with a large herd of Commerson's dolphins.

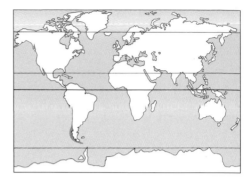

Communication—Sound emission. Low-level noises have been recorded in this species of a length of .4 to 2.0 seconds. They are similar to those of Hector's dolphin and Commerson's dolphin. No whistling has been recorded.

Distribution. This dolphin lives off the southern coast of Chile, from around Concepción to Tierra del Fuego (between 35° and 60° S).

31. COMMERSON'S DOLPHIN

Cephalorhynchus commersonii
(Lacépède, 1804)

Taxonomy. In the mid-eighteenth century, while going around the world in a boat, the French doctor and botanist P. Commerson observed a black-and-white dolphin in the Strait of Magellan. He described it in an unpublished report, which he gave to Buffon. In 1804 B. Lacépède named this cetacean *Delphinus commersonii*, in honor of the French doctor. Many dolphins of this species live by the shores of the Kerguelen Islands in the southern Indian Ocean. It is probably a geographic and genetic variant of the Chilean dolphin described above, differentiated by its larger size, its coloring, and its acoustic signalling.

Common names. France: Dauphin de Commerson, Jacobite, Céphalorhynque pie. Great Britain: Commerson's dolphin, Piebald dolphin. Latin America: Tunina orera, Delfin de Magallanes. Germany: Jacobitas, Commersondelphin. Japan: Panda iruka, Irokae iruka.

Description. Commerson's dolphin measures an average of 4 ft. 3 in. (1.30 m) and can reach 5 ft. 4 in. (1.65 m). It weighs between 88 and 110 lbs. (40 and 50 kg), with a maximum of 145 lbs. (66 kg). Newborns measure about 1 ft. 10 in. (60 cm) and weigh 20 to 22 lbs. (9 to 10 kg). The adult's body is small, robust, and spindle-shaped. The face is short and has a very reduced snout. There are 29 to 30 small cone-shaped teeth on each side of the jaws. The dorsal fin is short, low, slightly rounded, and median. The pectoral fins are small and somewhat rounded. The lower edge of the left pectoral fin is serrated in close to 80 percent of adult males and 36 percent of adult females. The right pectoral fin is rarely serrated. In newborns and young animals, this serration is completely absent. The caudal fin is crescent-shaped and has a median notch. The entire upper jaw and the upper part of the lower jaw, down to the pectoral fins, are black. A large band in pale grey to white spreads on the middle of the body between the back of the head and the front of the dorsal fin, covering the back, flanks, and stomach. The caudal peduncle is black, as are the dorsal and caudal fins. A white band runs along the chin, and there is a small black area around the anus. The genders are differentiated by size, the females being larger, and by the shape of the black spot in their anal region. The very young have a grey dorso-lateral cape, which disappears between the ages of one and two. The dolphins living in the Kerguelen Islands are approximately 20 percent larger than those living off the South

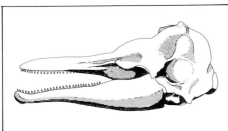

American coasts. The front and back parts of the animal are black, but they are separated by a lighter area. The grey dorsolateral cape found in juveniles remains in the Kerguelen variety.

Reproduction. Very little information is available on this animal's reproduction. Females reach sexual maturity towards the age of five, males towards the age of eight. The discovery of a fetus ready to be born in December in a female from Tierra del Fuego leads us to believe that the austral summer (December to April) is the birth season for this species. Gestation is

thought to last a year. A Commerson's dolphin was born in captivity at the San Diego Sea World in February 1985.

Population. This dolphin's population size is unknown. However, it is believed to be quite common around Tierra del Fuego. Off Argentina, almost 200 are accidentally captured each year in nets set out for crabs and some are intentionally caught in crab traps for human consumption and as bait. The flesh is also used in Chile as crab bait. Due to its small size and good adaptation to captivity, this dolphin is being captured for aquariums the world over. (It can be found at the Duisburg Zoo in Germany, Sunshine International Aquarium in Tokyo, and Sea World in San Diego.)

Diet. Commerson's dolphin mainly feeds on crustaceans (crabs and krill), small fish (sardines and anchovies), and cephalopods (octopus and cuttlefish), as well as on benthic invertebrates (isopods and scidiae). When in captivity, it eats between 7 and 9 lbs. (3 and 4 kg) of fish a day; the consumption of those living in the Kerguelen Islands is estimated at 11 lbs. (5 kg) a day.

Field identification. Commerson's dolphin is easy to recognize. When surfacing, the blowhole appears first, then the back, showing the dorsal fin; then it arches its back to dive back in immediately. This is not a shy dolphin; it plays in ships' bow waves, accompanies boats, and jumps completely out of the water when in their proximity. This cetacean generally emerges every 15 to 20 seconds and swims at a speed of 6 to 7 knots (11 to 17 km/hr). It can probably swim at 25 to 30 knots (46.3 to 55.6 km/hr) for short periods of time. It often switches direction underwater, and it is impossible to guess where it will emerge. An Argentinian zoologist counted that in 17 minutes six of these dolphins had jumped between 65 and 70 times. Commerson's dolphin usually swims in groups of two to 12, but sometimes up to 30 (in a group of 31 observed in Argentina, 11 were juveniles). Even larger groups have been observed. These groups are not permanent associations; rather, they are made and unmade in response to the situation.

Communication—Sound emission.
The population found in the Kerguelen Islands has two types of acoustical signal: mewings in a range of about 10 kHz with a dominant component at one kHz and echolocation clicks emitted in blasts of about 10 at a time. This dolphin does not produce whistles. The two main populations (South America and Kerguelen) have different echolocation clicks.

Distribution. Commerson's dolphin is a cold-water cetacean, frequenting the coastal waters at the southern tip of the South American continent (between 42° and 56° S). Its distribution zone includes the Argentine coast, from the Valdez peninsula to Tierra del Fuego, the area surrounding South Georgia, and the Falkland and Kerguelen islands.

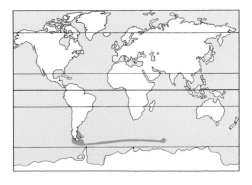

32. LONG-FINNED PILOT WHALE
Globicephala melaena
(Traill, 1809)

Taxonomy. In 1806 the Scottish doctor T. Traill collected a dolphin of this species from a herd of 92 that had been stranded on the Orkney Islands, north of Scotland. He called it *Delphinus melas,* from the Greek *melas,* black. In 1828 the Frenchman R. P. Lesson created the new genus *Globicephala,* from the Latin *globus,* globe, and the Greek *kephalos,* head, and put the dolphin described by Traill in it. It appears that the long-finned pilot whales living in the Northern Hemisphere differ from those living in the Southern Hemisphere, but they are still not divided into different species or subspecies. Further studies are being carried out on the Southern Hemisphere's population.

Common names. France: Dauphin pilote. Great Britain: Long-finned pilot whale. Germany: Langflossengrindwal. Latin America: Caldern negro, Ballena piloto. Japan: Magondo kujira.

Description. The male long-finned pilot whale measures an average of 20 ft. (6 m) and can reach 28 ft. (8.50 m). The female's average length is 16 ft. (5 m), and it can reach 20 ft. (6 m). Males can weigh more than 8,800 lbs. (4 metric tons) and females more than 4,400 lbs. (2 metric tons). Newborns measure 5 ft. 6 in. to 5 ft. 10 in. (1.70 to 1.80 m). This animal's body is long and sturdy, with a front that is more massive than the back. The peduncle is laterally compressed, especially in males, and both the upper and lower careens are accentuated in older animals. Its scientific name, *Globicephala,* is quite descriptive of the architecture of its head: A rounded frontal prominence dominates this animal's cephalic area and grows with age. The dorsal fin is rather low and extended (it is twice as long as it is high); it is falcate and placed a little ahead of the midpoint of the back. The flippers are up towards the front of the body; they are falcate and quite long (approximately one-fifth of the total body length). The flukes have a median notch. Newborns do not have any teeth, which appear when the dolphin reaches 7 ft. (2.13 m) and stop growing when it reaches 8 ft. 9 in. (2.70 m). Adults have eight to 10 big cone-shaped teeth approximately 2 in. (5 cm) long on each side of both jaws. This animal is generally black, with a dark grey mark on its back behind the dorsal fin and a small mark of the same color behind each ear. An anchor-shaped, pearly grey design is found on the ventral area between the throat and the anal region; it widens above the pectorals, narrows at their level, and widens again between the umbilical and anal regions.

Reproduction. The female's complete reproductive cycle takes three to five years. Females reach sexual maturity between the ages of six and seven (nine in Japan) when they have reached 12 ft., or 3.65 m, and males between the ages of 11 and 12 (17 in Japan) when they have reached 16 ft., or 4.90 m. Mating probably occurs year-round, but in the waters off Newfoundland it has been reported that much of it takes place between April and May. Gestation lasts 15 to 16 months, and most births occur during the summer, especially in August. Lactation lasts 21 to 22 months. Juveniles start taking in other food at six to nine months, when they measure 7 ft. 6 in. (2.30 m). Life expectancy is estimated at 46 to 50 years in females and 36 to 40 years in males.

Population. There used to be a population of long-finned pilot whales in the northern Pacific, which has now mysteriously vanished. In other parts of the world,

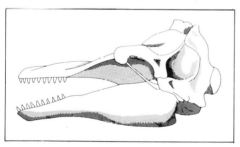

particularly in the northern Atlantic, it is still a common species, although its population has clearly diminished due to hunting, especially off the Faeroe Islands. There is no estimate of its total population. The hunt for these animals started in the Faeroe Islands, with about 1,500 animals caught each summer. The long-finned pilot whale population of that area can be numbered in the hundreds of thousands. It has also been hunted in the waters off the Orkney and Shetland islands and Newfoundland. In the summer of 1956, the

number of animals that were caught was 10,000, and, in 1961, it was 6,262. Some animals are also individually captured.

Diet. This animal's diet varies from one place to the next, depending on the prey's seasonal availability. It generally feeds on cephalopods, especially small octopus like *Illex illebrosus* in the northwest Atlantic, *Todarodes sagittatus* in European waters, *Gonatus fabricii* off the coast of Greenland, and *Loligo peali* in the Gulf of St. Lawrence. When octopus is rare, it eats, among other fish, herring and mullets. It eats 30 to 60 lbs., and even up to 75 lbs. (14 to 27 kg, and up to 35 kg) of food per day.

Field identification. The long-finned pilot whale remains at the surface for a number of minutes and breathes every one to two minutes. When it emerges, the enormous melon appears first, ejecting a blow up to 5 ft. (1.50 m) high, which is visible under any atmospheric conditions, even in the tropics. Then the back appears, showing the dorsal fin; close to three-fourths of the animal's length is visible. Before sounding, it arches its back and shows its tail. The long-finned pilot whale usually dives 100 to 200 ft. (30 to 60 m) deep in

122

search of food, but it can go farther, up to .625 miles (1 km)! It usually remains submerged for four to 10 minutes but can stay under up to two hours. It swims at a speed of 2 to 4 knots (3.7 to 7.4 km), sometimes 14 knots (26 km/hr), and, when terrified, it can reach a top speed of 25 knots (46 km/hr). This cetacean is indifferent to ships, although it occasionally remains in their proximity. Some individuals have been seen spy-hopping (raising their head vertically above the water as if supported on their flippers) and remaining immobile at the surface. The long-finned pilot whale occasionally swims with bottlenose and common dolphins. It is very gregarious and moves in groups of 10 to hundreds (a group of 3,000 has supposedly been observed). This animal is totally nonaggressive. There have been mass strandings of this species throughout the world with more than 50, and sometimes more than 100, individuals per stranding.

Communication—Sound emission.
The long-finned pilot whale emits all sorts of sounds: creakings, whistles,

snapping noises, snores, mewings, hummings, and gurgles. Most of these sound emissions have a social purpose

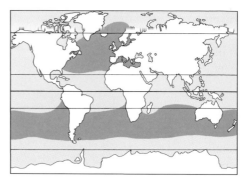

and are used to communicate, although some are used for echolocation.

Distribution. In the Northern Hemisphere, this dolphin lives on both sides of the Atlantic Ocean, the European and the American. In the Southern Hemisphere, it is only found in cold and temperate waters. This dolphin apparently migrates seasonally, due to water temperatures and probably also prey availability.

33. SHORT-FINNED PILOT WHALE
Globicephalus macrorhynchus
(Gray, 1846)

Taxonomy. J. E. Gray described a few new species of *Globicephala* in 1846, including one from "the South Seas," which he named *Globicephalus macrorhynchus*, from the Greek *makros*, long or large, and *rhynchos*, nose or beak. The Southern Hemisphere population seems quite different from the population in the Northern Hemisphere, and has much longer flippers. Some researchers consider this population a separate species or subspecies, but at this time zoological nomenclature does not recognize it as such. There are also two other visibly distinct geographic types off the Pacific coast of Japan, to the north and south.

Common names. Great Britain: Short-finned pilot whale, Blackfish, Pothead. Latin America: Calderon, Ballena piloto. Russia: Grinda. Germany: Kurzflossen-grindwal. Japan: Kobire gondo kujira, Shio gondo kijura (Southern Hemisphere population).

Description. The male short-finned pilot whale measures 18 ft. to 20 ft. (5.50 to 6 m) on an average and a maximum of 22 ft. (6.70 m). For females, the average is 13 ft. to 15 ft. (4 to 4.50 m), and they can go over 16 ft. (5 m). Newborns measure 4 ft. 4 in. to 4 ft. 7 in. (1.35 to 1.45 m). The adult's body morphology is identical to

that of the long-finned pilot whale. Both have a long and sturdy body, with a predominant melon that develops with age. The dorsal fin is falcate, short, and extended (twice as long as it is high), and it is placed ahead of the midpoint of the body. The pectoral fins are falcate and shorter than in the long-finned pilot whale, since they are only one-sixth the length of the body. The flukes have a median notch. There are seven to nine large cone-shaped teeth on each half-jaw (eight to 12 for the population of the Southern Hemisphere). The body is generally black, with a grey anchor-shaped stain from the chin to the anus. This does not appear on the population of the Southern Hemisphere.

Reproduction. The female's complete reproductive cycle lasts three years. In the waters off South Africa, the female reaches sexual maturity upon measuring about 10 ft. (3 to 3.20 m), at the age of six. The male is sexually mature at 14 ft. to 15 ft. (4.30 to 4.40 m), between the ages of 10 and 11. Various researchers attribute different durations to the gestation

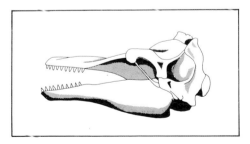

period, with estimates running from 11 to 13 months and from 15 to 16 months.

Population. We do not have any data on this animal's total global population, but we do know that it is common within its distribution area. Its numbers could be reduced by Japanese exploitation. In 1983 they reported 2,563 animals caught by commercial fishermen (approximately 800 are caught each year off Okinawa and the Izu peninsula) and 133 accidentally caught by various nets and in seines. In the eastern central Pacific, the population is estimated at about 60,000, but some are also caught there in nets. As many as 200 to 300 are harpooned to death each year off St. Vincent in the Caribbean.

Diet. Like the long-finned pilot whale, the short-finned pilot whale feeds mostly on octopus. The stomach contents of animals living off South Africa included the beaks of different octopus species, such as *Loligo reynaudi* and *Oregoniateuthis*. Off

southern California, this species eats *Loligo opalescens,* and, along the west African coast, it swims with tuna to gorge on *Illex illecebrosus coindeti.* The stomach remains of animals living in the Caribbean include both octopus and fish. In this region, it also swims with tuna, probably in order to hunt. Daily consumption for the short-finned pilot whale is 44 to 99 lbs. (20 to 45 kg) of food a day.

Field identification. The short-finned pilot whale's behavior is identical to that of the long-finned pilot whale. It can reach a depth of close to 2,000 ft. (600 m) and has been recorded at depths even beyond that. It swims with the Pacific white-sided dolphin and the bottlenose dolphin, and it moves in herds of 40 to a few hundred. There have been mass strandings of this species throughout the world, with a certain number concentrated on the shores of Senegal. The number of animals per stranding varies from 22 (Venezuela, October 1971) to 151 (Senegal, May 1943).

Communication—Sound emission.
This cetacean emits many sounds, such as whistles and snapping noises, and seems to have the same repertory of sounds as the long-finned pilot whale.

Distribution. This animal frequents all of the tropical and temperate waters of the Atlantic, Pacific, and Indian oceans. Its seasonal migration is not yet well known.

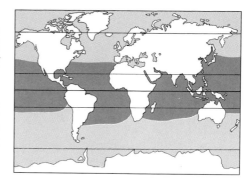

34. KILLER WHALE
Orcinus orca
(Linnacus, 1758)

Taxonomy. It was C. Linnaeus who described this enormous animal from the stories of sailors. He named it *Delphinus orca,* the demon dolphin. In 1860 it was placed in the new genus *Orcinus*. We do not know the exact translation of its scientific name. According to some sources, it comes from the Latin *orca,* a whale breed, or from *orcynus,* a tuna breed. At present, only a single breed is recognized in zoological nomenclature within the genus *Orcinus*, although recent studies prove that

certain populations of killer whales are anatomically different enough from *Orcinus orca* to warrant the creation of new species or subspecies. For instance, in 1981, Soviet researchers noted the existence of a dwarfish variety living in the Southern Hemisphere and named it *Orcinus nanus;* however, its status in zoological nomenclature has not yet been confirmed due to lack of information. That same year, other Russian researchers described another variety (which could be the same as the preceding one), which they named the glacial killer whale *(Orcinus glacialis),* and which lives in Arctic waters of the same longitude as the Indian Ocean. It appears that there are other geographic varieties

126

not yet discovered. Such may be the case with the seven large killer whales, measuring between 19 ft. 6 in. and 29 ft. 6 in. (6 and 9 m), observed in Antarctic waters in January and February of 1902, which had a very high dorsal fin. Other animals resembling this description were seen in 1910 and 1911, also in the waters of Antarctica. Morzer Bruyns refers to another sort of killer whale living in the eastern part of the Gulf of Aden that measures 19 ft. 6 in. to 23 ft. (6 to 7 m) at a weight estimated to be 4,000 lbs. (1,800 kg); he named this animal Alula whale or Alula killer. The killer whale has a very diversified geographic distribution, and it is possible that within a few years some subspecies, if not some outright new species, will be described.

Common names. France: Epaulard. Great Britain: Killer whale, Orca, Great killer whale. Russia: Kosatka. Germany: Schwertwal. Japan: Syachi, Sakamata. Latin America: Orca, Ballena asesina.

Description. The male killer whale measures 26 ft. to 29 ft. 6 in. (8 to 9 m) on an average, with a maximum of 32 ft. (9.75 m). The female measures from 23 ft. to 25 ft. (7 to 7.70 m) and can reach 28 ft. (8.5 m). As for the dwarfish form discovered by the Russian scientists in the Southern Hemisphere *(O. nanus)*, the male measures a maximum of 24 ft. 6 in. (7.50 m) and the female 21 ft. (6.50 m). The male can weigh up to 18,000 lbs. (8.2 metric tons) and the female 8,800 lbs. (4 metric tons). In general, the male killer whale weighs 1,400 lb./yd. (700 kg/m) and the female 1,000 lb./yd. (500 kg/m). Newborns measure 6 ft. 6 in. to 7 ft. 9 in. (2 to 2.40 m) (9 ft., or 2.76 m) and weigh about 400 lbs. (180 kg). The adult's general morphology is strong and spindle-shaped. The head is big, somewhat cone-shaped,

with a rounded forehead and no rostrum. Each half-jaw sports 10 to 13 large cone-shaped teeth (with an average diameter of 25 to 50 mm at the gum level). The dorsal fin is median, that of females and juveniles is falcate, and it is about 2 ft. 9 in. (90 cm) high in females. The male's dorsal fin is straight and higher —5 ft. 6 in. to 6 ft. 6 in. (1.70 to 2 m). The flippers are racket-shaped, wide, and rounded. The flukes account for about 20 percent of the total body length; a median notch is present. The body's coloring varies by herd and habitat. The back and flanks are usually black, and the ventral area is white from the chin to the anus, extending laterally onto the flanks towards the back. There is a white mark above and behind each eye. The fins are all black, although the ventral area of the flukes is white. A grey, saddle-shaped mark is found behind the dorsal fin. Young individuals are greyish in areas that are black in adults and a fawn color in the white areas. Each animal is unique due to the morphology of its dorsal fin and to its markings. This recent discovery has made

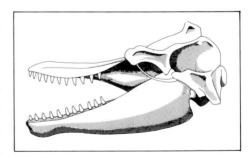

it possible to estimate certain endemic populations and to follow the organization and evolution of this species long-term.

Reproduction. The female killer whale's complete reproductive cycle lasts more than two years (possibly three to eight). Males reach sexual maturity upon

measuring 21 ft. 9 in. (6.70 m), and females when they reach 16 ft. (5 m). Mating and births seem to take place year-round, although copulations are concentrated from spring to the beginning of summer (May to July). Gestation lasts 12 to 16 months. Most births occur in the fall and early winter, and the newborn is weaned in a year. There has been a lot of discussion regarding the life expectancy of these animals. Studies based on the life of a killer whale known as Old Tom in the waters of Western Australia's Twofold Bay have confirmed that it was 35 at the time of its death, rather than 50 or 90, as had previously been suggested. It is believed that the life expectancy is 60 to 80 years for females and 50 years for males. The life expectancy of a killer whale in captivity is three to six years.

Population. We have no estimates of the total global population for the killer whale, but we know that this species is relatively common, particularly in zones up to 500 miles (800 km) from the coast in the cold waters of both hemispheres. There are, however, estimates for certain areas of the world. In Antarctica, for example, there appear to be more than 160,000 killer whales. A recent study in which animals were identified by their coloring counted the number of killer whales around Vancouver and found 330, rather than the thousands that had been estimated before. The killer whale is far from being an endangered species, although it is uselessly slaughtered in certain parts of the world. This is especially the case in Norway (where 250 animals were captured in 1970), in Japan (where about 50 are captured per year), and in Korea and Iceland (where this cetacean is commercially fished). Thousands of killer whales were captured by the USSR in Antarctica in 1979. Aquariums have been interested in this species since 1961, when Pacific Marineland in Palo Verdes, California,

128

captured a female lost in Newport Harbor by net. Unfortunately, it only lived for a day and a half in captivity. In 1962 the same aquarium caught another adult female that died during its capture in Puget Sound in Washington State. In 1964 a young male was captured in British Co lumbia, Canada, and transferred to a pond, where it survived for three months. Since then, a killer-whale fishery has been organized in British Columbia and Washington State. In that region alone, 647 killer whales were captured between 1962 and 1973 in response to the needs of North American aquariums. The populations in this area were diminishing and not reconstituting themselves due to these captures. It thus became necessary to stop and capture these whales somewhere else, such as off Iceland. The first killer whale captured there, in 1976, was Kim, a female measuring 14 ft. 8 in. (4.50 m) that was kept in the Marineland of Antibes. Occasionally, killer whales are caught by the Japanese off their shores for aquariums.

Diet. The killer whale is at the top of the marine world's feeding chain. It is voracious and its nutritional choices seem limitless (cephalopods, birds, fish, reptiles, and marine mammals of all sizes). However, studies carried out in Japan prove that two-thirds of the stomach contents of this species are composed of fish and octopus. The fish most often consumed are cod, sardines, tuna, and salmon. Reference is often made to the discovery of 13 dolphins and 15 seals in the stomach of a single killer whale, but this information must be regarded with some reservations. When in groups, the killer whale attacks large cetaceans, but rarely healthy individuals. Captive killer whales consume 55 to 175 lbs. (25 to 80 kg) of food a day.

Field identification. It is easy to identify killer whales due to their dorsal fin and ·

general coloring. They go through three to five short emersions, 10 to 30 seconds apart, in a row and then dive for one to four minutes. A 14 minute immersion has been recorded (the animal was swimming at 12.5 mph, or 20 km/hr, at the time) as well as one 21 minutes long (this whale was diving at a depth of almost 1,000 ft, or 290 m). The breath is noisy and characterized by a blow that is 4 ft. 9 in. to 14 ft. 6 in. (1.50 to 4.50 m) high. This whale usually swims at a cruising speed of 4 knots (7.4 km/hr) and can reach a top speed of 30 knots (50 km/hr). It is generally indifferent to ships; it lets them approach and is totally nonaggressive, although a small number of reports suggest the contrary. When at the surface, the

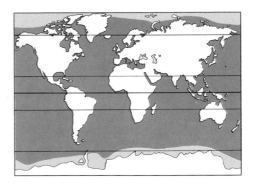

killer whale indulges in all sorts of behavior, such as lob-tailing and spy-hopping. Couples and single individuals are often sighted; however, this is generally a gregarious animal that swims in small communities of about 25 or 30 to several hundred animals, particularly off Iceland. Within a group, usually 20 percent are males and 20 percent are very young, with the rest of the group composed of females and immature males. The group structure is highly organized. Mass strandings have occurred throughout the world (Scotland, Sri Lanka, Canada, New Zealand, Australia, Argentina and Norway), but particularly in New Zealand. The number of whales in a mass stranding can exceed 100 (there were 150 in Scotland in 1927 and 160 in Sri Lanka in 1929).

Communication—Sound emission.
The killer whale makes all sorts of sounds of both low and high frequencies. Clicks of a frequency ranging from .25 to 35 kHz and shrieks of 2 kHz have been recorded by this species. While studying various groups around Vancouver with hydrophones, the Canadian J. K. Ford discovered that each group has its own unique dialect composed of acoustic signals that are different from those of other groups.

Distribution. The killer whale has a broad distribution and frequents both coastal and oceanic waters from Arctica to Antarctica.

35. FALSE KILLER WHALE
Pseudorca crassidens
(Owen, 1846)

Taxonomy. The British paleontologist R. Owen described the first specimen of this species in 1846 from a pseudo-fossil skeleton discovered in Great Britain, and named it *Phocaena crassidens*, from the Latin *crassus*, thick, and *dens*, tooth. Sixteen years later, a hundred or so of these dolphins were stranded in Kiel Bay in Germany. The German biologist J. Reinhardt examined a few of them and concluded that this was the cetacean described by Owen. Reinhardt created a new genus, *Pseudorca*, from the Greek *pseudo*, false, and the Latin *orca*, probably a type of whale (see the Killer Whale).

Common names. France: Faux orque, Pseudorque. Great Britain: False killer whale. Latin America: Orca falsa. Russia: Malaya, Chornaya, Kosatya. Germany: Falscher, Unechter, Schwarzer oder mittlerer schwertwal. Japan: Oki gondo kujira.

Description. The false killer whale measures an average of 18 ft. (5.50 m) for males and 15 ft. (4.60 m) for females; the maximum length is 19 ft. 6 in. (6 m) for males and 17 ft. 7 in. (5.40 m) for females. The male's maximum weight is 4,840 lbs. (2.2 metric tons), and the maximum weight of the female is 2,420 lbs. (1.1 metric ton). The newborn measures 4 ft. 9 in. to 5 ft. 10 in. (1.50 to 1.80 m). The adult's body is long, and its head has an elongated profile. The top jaw is longer than the bottom one. Each half-jaw sports seven to 11 teeth. The dorsal fin is falcate, of medium height (about eight percent of the total body length), and right behind the

midpoint of the animal. The flippers are short, and there is a bump about halfway along the back of the fin. The flukes have a median notch. The false killer whale is completely black, except for a grey area between the pectorals on the ventral side.

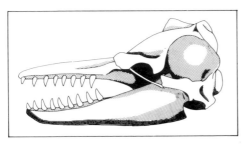

Reproduction. We know little about this animal's reproduction. Mating and birth occur year-round. Males and females reach sexual maturity between the ages of eight and 14 at 13 ft. to 15 ft. (3.95 to 4.55 m) for males and 12 ft. to 14 ft. (3.60 to 4.25 m) for females. Gestation probably lasts about 15 months, and lactation about 18. There have been a few cases of hybridization with the bottlenose dolphin in captivity (Kamogawa Sea World in Japan and Sea Life Park in Hawaii).

Population. The false killer whale is relatively abundant within its distribution area, although we lack an estimate of its total global population. In Japan, herds of this cetacean are cornered, driven towards shore, and slaughtered. This particularly occurs on the island of Iki. Between April 1976 and January 1982, as many as 953 false killer whales were killed in this manner. This cetacean is also killed for other reasons than its flesh. According to the Japanese, it competes with fishermen and reduces the number of fish in the region. However, studies conducted on its dietary habits have not included an appraisal of this competition. It is not only in Japan that this species attacks tuna; similar cases

have been reported in the east central Pacific, where about 10 individuals are captured each year off Hawaii and Australia. At St. Vincent in the Caribbean, these animals are occasionally captured. In Japan, some of the animals that are caught are spared so as to be transported to aquariums.

Diet. The false killer whale's diet is heavy in octopus (the beaks of 11 of these cephalopods were found in the stomach of a single individual off the coast of South Africa) as well as large fish. It attacks large pelagic fish, such as Coryhaenidae and Scombridae. Fishermen often report having seen false killer whales attack dolphins as they are let out of tuna nets in the tropical east Pacific.

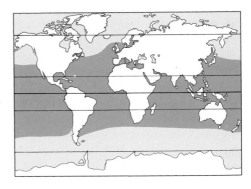

Field identification. As soon as a false killer whale surfaces to breathe, three-fourths of its head appears above water. It then shows its entire back and part of its flanks. Adults breathe every 12 to 20 seconds, and the young every eight seconds on an average. The false killer whale sometimes approaches ships and plays in the bow waves for a few minutes, despite its slow speed when compared to other dolphins. It swims at a cruising speed of 2 to 3 knots (3.7 to 5.5 km/hr), and its peak speed is thought to be 15 knots (27.8 km/

hr). It sometimes jumps completely out of the water, hitting the surface of the sea with its tail (lob tailing). This is a gregarious animal, with strong social bonds. Small groups of two to about 20 animals are usually observed, but it is not rare for herds to number over a hundred. The false killer whale holds the record for a mass stranding: 800 individuals on the Argentinian coast in 1964. The major mass strandings have occurred on the coasts of Great Britain, New Zealand, Tasmania, South Australia, South Africa, and Florida. This appears to be the primary cause of mortality for this species. Some of these animals have been observed swimming in the company of Risso's dolphins. The false killer whale is sought after by aquariums because it adapts relatively well to captivity.

Communication—Sound emission.
This species emits a surprisingly diverse array of sounds. It appears that each individual produces a different sound, or, to quote James Porter of the University of Michigan, "You get the feeling that they aren't all saying the same thing at the same time." Since this is a highly gregarious cetacean, communication plays an important role in maintaining social cohesion. It also emits sounds for echolocation.

Distribution. The false killer whale is a pelagic and widespread cetacean that favors tropical and temperate waters. We do not know if this species migrates on a seasonal basis, other than its travels to the coast in search of food.

36. PYGMY KILLER WHALE
Feresa attenuata
(Gray, 1874)

Taxonomy. The British naturalist Gray described the pygmy killer whale in 1827, from a skull of unknown origin, under the name *Delphinus intermedius*. In 1871 he suggested a new genus, *Feresa* (possibly from the old French vernacular for dolphin) and named the species *F. attenuata,* from the Latin word for reduced. Some individuals were found stranded in Senegal, Namibia, and South Africa, and a herd of 14 was captured in Futo (Shizuoka prefecture, Japan) in 1963, allowing us to have a better understanding of this animal.

Common names. France: Orque naine. Great Britain: Pygmy killer whale, Slender pilot whale, Slender blackfish. Latin America: Orca pigméo. Germany: Zwergschwertwal. Russia: Karlikovaya kasatka. Japan: Yume gondo kujira.

Description. The male pygmy killer whale measures an average of 7 ft. to 7 ft. 6 in. (2.20 to 2.30 m) and a maximum of 9 ft. (2.75 m). The female measures 6 ft. 9 in. (2.13 m) on an average and can reach 7 ft. 10 in. (2.40 m). The male adult's average weight is 375 lbs. (170 kg), and the female's is 330 lbs. (150 kg), with a maximum of 500 lbs. (225 kg) for the male and 440 lbs. (200 kg) for the female. Newborns measure 1 ft. 6 in. to 2 ft. 8 in. (50 to 85 cm). This whale has a slender body, with a laterally compressed and somewhat stocky posterior half. The rounded head has a convex, elongated profile, with an upper jaw that is longer than the lower, and without a snout. Each side of the upper jaw has eight to 12 teeth, while there are 10 to 13 on each side of the lower jaw. The dorsal fin is median, falcate or triangular, and high. The long, wide-based flippers can measure up to 20 or 23 percent of the total body length, and the flukes have a median slit. There is a narrow furrow on the ventral side, between the inferior thoracic region and the genital orifice. These animals are black or dark grey, with flanks that are often lighter. There is a lighter ventral area between the pectoral fins and a long white mark running from the stomach to the anal region. The lips are white.

Reproduction. We know very little about this animal's reproduction. Two gestating females captured in Japan measuring 7 ft. 2 in. and 7 ft. 5 in. (2.21 and 2.27 m) and a male measuring 7 ft. (2.16 m) were sexually mature; thus, about 7 ft. 2 in. (2.20 m) is probably the length at which males and females reach sexual maturity. The birth season is thought to take place in the spring and summer.

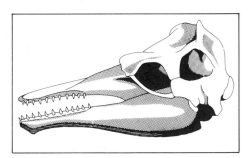

Population. We have no estimate of the pygmy killer whale's total population. However, during the past 20 years, herds and strandings have been observed almost throughout its distribution area, which leads us to believe that it is not quite as rare as was previously thought. Some individuals have been caught in tuna nets in the tropical Pacific, and a herd has been caught in the Iru peninsula in Japan. A few are caught in fishing expeditions from St. Vincent in the Caribbean.

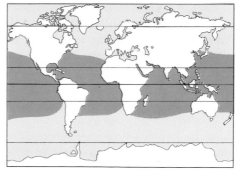

Diet. This animal's diet is not quite clear to us. The stomach remains of a specimen stranded on the coast of South Africa contained cephalopod beaks. One animal in captivity at the Hawaii Sea Life Park consumed 14 to 22 lbs. (6.5 to 10 kg) of octopus, mackerel, and other small fish per day. In Japan, a female refused octopus, mackerel, and other small fish to feed exclusively on about 18 lbs. (8 kg) of sardines per day. Since the pygmy killer whale has demonstrated aggressive behavior towards other cetacean species when in captivity, it is possible that it also feeds on marine mammals and birds.

Field identification. When surfacing, the pygmy killer whale's head comes completely out of the water. This species breathes every six to seven seconds, usually three to four times per minute, and remains underwater from 25 seconds to

three minutes. Its cruising speed is 6 knots (11 km/hr), and it can reach a peak speed of over 20 knots (37 km/hr). The pygmy killer whale plays in the bow waves of ships and sometimes rests by staying immobile at the surface of the water. Some individuals have been seen sky-hopping, that is, holding their body vertically in the water and their head out to the base of their flippers. This dolphin does not jump out of the water, but it does lob-tail, slapping the surface with its tail. In captivity, it is aggressive towards other cetaceans and towards trainers. At Sea Life Park, a pygmy killer whale killed a young pilot whale, and the species has been seen attacking small cetaceans in the South Atlantic and tropical Pacific oceans. It is a gregarious animal and swims in herds of about 10, or even 50, to many hundreds strong. It has been seen swimming with Fraser's dolphins. There have been some mass strandings of the pygmy killer whale. Five were found stranded in South Africa in January 1968.

Communication—Sound emission.
We have no data on the communication and sound emission skills or habits for this species.

Distribution. The pygmy killer whale lives in the temperate and tropical waters of the Pacific, Atlantic, and Indian oceans. It does not appear to migrate, remaining instead in the same regions year-round.

37. MELON-HEADED WHALE
Peponocephala electra
(Gray, 1846)

Taxonomy. J. E. Gray described this species in 1846 from his observations of two skulls, thinking that they were part of the *Lagenorhynchus* genus. This cetacean was then studied in Hawaii in 1966 and given the genus name *Peponocephala,* from the Greek *pepon,* gourd or melon, and *kephalos,* head. *Electra* is a character from Greek mythology, a nymph and the daughter of Ocean and Tethys.

Common names. France: Dauphin d'Electre. Great Britain: Melon-headed whale, Little killer whale, Many-toothed black fish. Germany: Melonenkopf. Russia: Shiroku klyuvyy del'fin. Japan: Kazuha gondo kujira.

Description. The melon-headed whale measures 7 ft. (2.20 m) on an average but can reach 9 ft. (2.70 to 2.80 m). Its weight varies between 350 and 375 lbs. (160 and 170 kg) and can reach 440 lbs. (200 kg). The newborn probably measures between 3 ft. and 4 ft. (90 and 120 cm). This animal has a long and fusiform body, and its head is more pointed than that of the pygmy killer whale. There is no rostrum. Each side of the upper jaw sports 20 to 25 small, pointed teeth, and each side of the lower jaw sports 22 to 24. The dorsal fin is median, falcate, extended, and rather high (it can reach a height of almost 1 ft., or 30 cm). The flippers are relatively short and about 20 percent of the total body length. The flukes have a median notch. The body is black or dark grey, except for the noticeably lighter stomach and genital parts, and the areas between the pectoral fins and close to the anus, which are grey or white. There is also a small grey or white lip line.

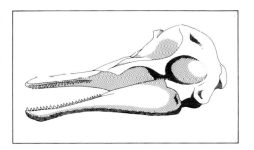

Reproduction. We have very little information on the melon-headed whale's reproduction. Males probably reach sexual maturity when measuring 7 ft. (2.26 m), and females when they measure 7 ft. to 8 ft. (2.25 to 2.50 m). According to data collected on stranded animals in the Southern Hemisphere, the reproductive season seems to take place during the austral summer (August to December); indeed, many newborns and pregnant females have been seen among stranded animals during the months of July and August. Gestation is thought to last 12 months.

Population. We cannot estimate the melon-headed whale's total population, but it does not seem particularly rare, especially in the Pacific. A few individuals are captured in tuna nets in the tropical

oriental Pacific. In 1965, as many as 250 of a herd of 500 were driven towards the shore in the Suruga Bay, in Japan, and slaughtered. In 1979, 150 melon-headed whales were captured by a Japanese fishery. Some have been caught by fisheries in St. Vincent, in the Caribbean. The flesh of animals of this species stranded on the Australian coast was used as bait in crab traps.

Diet. The stomach contents of animals captured at St. Vincent revealed fish oto-

liths, octopus beaks, isopods, and a very large red shrimp. In South Africa, the beaks of *Loligo reynaudi* and hake *(Merlucius sp.)* otoliths were found in the stomach of some of these whales.

Field identification. The melon-headed whale creates a lot of foam as it comes above the water surface to breathe, which it does every 10 to 20 seconds, swimming at a speed of 2 to 3 knots (3.7 to 5.5 km/hr). Its top speed is 15 knots (27.8 km/hr).

It sometimes jumps completely out of the water and often plays in the bow waves of ships. But it is still difficult to approach. Some melon-headed whales were observed attacking a dolphin of the Stenella genus as it was being freed from tuna nets, but they may have been confused with pygmy killer whales. This is a very gregarious animal, which travels in groups of five to 30, sometimes even 200 to 500. Most of the information we have on this species comes to us from mass strandings, such as

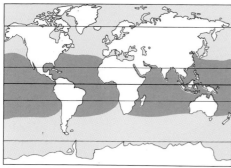

Communication—Sound emission. At this point, there is no data on sound emission for this species.

Distribution. The melon-headed whale frequents the tropical and subtropical waters of the Atlantic, Pacific, and Indian oceans. This species is not well enough known for us to be aware of any possible migration.

one that occurred in Australia (between 150 and 250 individuals in August 1958).

38. HARBOR PORPOISE
Phocoena phocoena
(Linnaeus, 1758)

Taxonomy. The harbor porpoise was the most common cetacean off the European coasts during the eighteenth century. Linnaeus described it in 1758 under the name *Delphinus phocoena*, from the Greek *phokaina* or the Latin *phocaena*, for porpoise, and G. Cuvier established the genus *Phocoena*.

Common names. Great Britain: Common porpoise, Harbor porpoise. Germany: Kleintümmler, Schweinswal, "Braunfisch." Russia: Morskaya svin'ya. Japan: Nezumi iruka.

Description. The harbor porpoise measures 5 ft. (1.50 to 1.60 m) on an average, but its maximum length can be over 6 ft. 6 in. (2 m). Its average weight varies between 100 and 130 lbs. (45 and 60 kg), but it can reach 200 lbs. (90 kg). Newborns measure between 2 ft. and 3 ft. (70 and 90 cm) and weigh 11 to 22 lbs. (5 to 10 kg). The harbor porpoise's body is short and stocky; the head is short, truncated, and lacking a snout. There are 22 to 28 short teeth with flattened ends on each of the four half-jaws. The dorsal fin is a little to the back of the body's midpoint, and it is low and triangular with a slightly concave front edge. The flippers are oval, short, and wide. The flukes have a median notch. The caudal peduncle is careened. The body is usually dark grey, with light grey marks on the flanks and white ones on

the stomach. A grey line joins the mouth's commissure to the base of the flippers. The fins are dark grey.

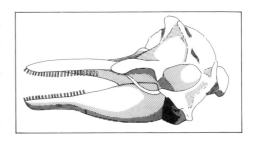

Reproduction. The reproductive cycle of the harbor porpoise lasts 24 months. Males and females become sexually mature between the ages of three and four. At that point, males measure from 3 ft. 11 in. to 4 ft. 3 in. (1.20 to 1.30 m) and females measure about 4 ft. 6 in. (1.40 m). The birth and mating seasons vary greatly with each population. The mating season is either from August to September in north European waters; from June to August in waters off Great Britain and the Nether- Bay of Fundy in Canada, and the northwest coast of the United States; or from July to August in the west Baltic Sea. Gestation is thought to last eight to 11 months. Births occur during the spring (between March and July in the waters of Norway), at the end of spring, or at the beginning of summer (between May and June for the Pacific Northwest). Juveniles start eating solid food at five months and are weaned at eight months. Life expectancy is estimated at six to 12 years.

Population. A few centuries ago, this species was fairly common in European

waters. Over the past few years, however, the number of individuals in the European Atlantic and in the Baltic and North seas has diminished for unknown reasons. The harbor porpoise is regularly, though accidentally, captured throughout its distribution area. It has been exploited in Japan and the Black Sea, which helps to explain its rarity; furthermore, over 1,000 individuals are captured annually in Iceland and Greenland.

Diet. The harbor porpoise mostly eats nonspiny fish, and has a particular predilection for Gadoidae and Clupeiodae. Herring, sardines, mackerel, cod, sole, and hake, as well as cephalopods and crustaceans are generally found in its stomach. It eats 6.5 to 11 lbs. (3 to 5 kg) of food per day.

Field identification. The harbor por-poise's small size makes it difficult to observe in its natural habitat. When it emerges to breathe, only the back and dorsal fin appear above water level. When it is moving, the harbor porpoise breathes every 15 seconds, but when it is feeding, it surfaces three or four times to breathe at intervals of two to three minutes. It remains submerged between three and six minutes but can last up to 12 minutes. One individual was accidentally caught in a net at a depth of 260 ft. (79 m). This porpoise is a slow swimmer, but a top speed of 12 knots (22.2. km) has been recorded. The harbor porpoise is a shy animal that avoids contact with swimmers and ships and takes off at the slightest provocation. It does not jump out of the water, nor does it play in the bow waves of ships. When there is a calm sea, it floats on the water, where it can be more easily approached. It is a gregarious species that travels in couples or in small groups of five to 10, although herds of about a hundred are seen. The herds are usually separated by gender: adult males on one side, adult females and their young on the other.

Communication—Sound emission.

The harbor porpoise's sound emissions are low-intensity and made up of either a single click or by pulses resulting from more than 1,000 clicks per second. These sounds have a frequency of 2 kHz and are mostly used for echolocation.

Distribution. The harbor porpoise is a coastal cetacean that favors the cold waters of the north Atlantic and Pacific oceans (under 60 °F, or 15 °C). Yet it is found in

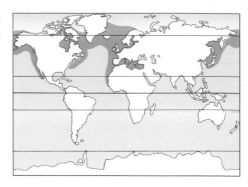

the Mediterranean and North seas, which is still not understood. It sometimes enters rivers. This is a migratory cetacean that spends the winter in the southern part of its area of distribution and goes north during the summer.

39. BURMEISTER'S PORPOISE

Phocoena spinipinnis
(Burmeister, 1865)

Taxonomy. In 1865 some fishermen captured a porpoise of this species at the mouth of the Rio de la Plata. The German entomologist H. Burmeister, who was then the director of the Buenos Aires Natural History Museum, described it under the species name *spinipinnis,* from the Latin *spinna,* with spines, and *pinnis,* wing or fin, because of the strange morphology of its dorsal fin.

Common names. France: Marsouin noir. Great Britain: Burmeister's porpoise, Black porpoise. Latin America: Marsopa espinosa, Chanco marino. Germany: Schwarzer tümmler, Burmeister's tümmler. Japan: Kohari iruka.

Description. Burmeister's porpoise measures 5 ft. (1.50 m) on an average but can reach 6 ft. 3 in. (1.90 m). Its average weight is 110 lbs. (50 kg), with a maximum estimated at 175 lbs. (80 kg). The adult's body is as stocky as that of the harbor porpoise, but the head is not as round. A triangular dorsal fin characterizes

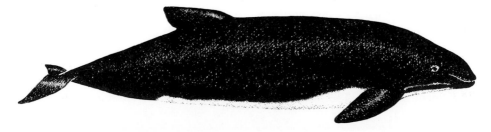

this species. Placed behind the median body point, it is slightly concave in the back, and its anterior edge sports about half a dozen spiny tubercles arranged in three rows. The flippers are relatively large and paddle-shaped. Older animals have an upper and lower careen on the caudal peduncle, right at the base of the tail. There are 14 to 16 teeth on each side of the upper jaw and 17 to 19 on each side of the lower jaw. The body is dark grey or black. There is a small light grey area on the stomach and, on some individuals, a light grey, mottled mark around the anus. There is also a white area, starting from the tip of the lower jaw and running to the anterior end of the flippers.

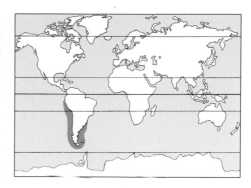

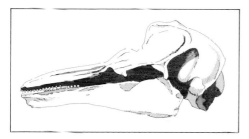

Reproduction. We have little data on this porpoise's reproduction. A well-formed fetus, measuring 1 ft. 5 in. (44 cm), probably ready for birth, was found in a female captured off the coast of Uruguay at the end of February.

Population. Burmeister's porpoise is not well known. It was long thought to be rare, although South American zoologists consider it the most common cetacean off the coasts of Chile and Argentina. We have no idea of its total numbers, but there are apparently two stocks of this porpoise: the Atlantic South American coast and the Pacific South American coast. This species is often caught in the nets used for shark hunting off the coast of Uruguay. It

is believed to be exploited on the Pacific coast of South America, especially in Peru, where it gets caught in nets intended for Scianidae. Approximately 2,000 individuals are caught each year to be sold on the Peruvian market. Chilean fishermen use it as bait and probably also as food. The repercussions of these captures are not known.

Diet. All we know of this animal's dietary habits comes from the stomach contents of a Uruguayan specimen, which was composed of fish (*Merluccius hubbsi* and *Pagrus sedecim*) and an unidentified octopus.

Field identification. Unfortunately, few observations of Burmeister's porpoise have been carried out in their natural habitat. In the Gulf of San Jose (Chubut, Argentina), it was observed swimming at a speed of 2 to 2.5 mph (3 to 4 km/hr) and immersing two or three times for 30 to 50 seconds each time, and then immersing for 1 minute to 3 minutes 20 seconds. According to Morzer Bruyns, this porpoise can reach a speed of 8 knots (14.8 km/hr) and breathes every five to 15 seconds. The Chilean cetologist A. L. Aguayo observed a group of eight individuals at the mouth of the river Lao in October 1965.

142

Communication—Sound emission. We do not have any data for this species on this topic.

Distribution. Burmeister's porpoise frequents the coastal waters of South America, from the tip of Devil's Point in Uruguay to Tierra del Fuego on the Atlantic side and from Peru to Chile on the Pacific side. This cetacean swims by the coasts during the spring, summer, and fall, and goes farther out to sea in the winter.

40. VAQUITA
Phocoena sinus
(Norris and McFarland, 1958)

Taxonomy. The American zoologist K. Norris found a skull from this species on the Punta San Felipe beach in the Gulf of California in 1950. He later published a description of this small cetacean with W. McFarland, based on the study of more skulls. The name comes from the Latin *sinus*, bay, due to its distribution in the Gulf of California.

Common names. France: Marsouin du Golfe de Californie, Marsoun du Pacifique. Great Britain: Cochito, Gulf porpoise, Gulf of California harbor porpoise. Germany: Golftümmler. Russia: Kaliforniyskaya morskaya svin'ya. Latin America: Vaquita, Cochito. Japan: Kogarashi nezumi iruka.

Description. Although this cetacean was first described more than 30 years ago, very few specimens have been examined since. The vaquita measures between 4 ft. and 5 ft. (1.30 and 1.50 m); the male measures a maximum of 4 ft. 6 in. (1.40 m), and the female a maximum of 5 ft. (1.50 m). Adults weigh between 75 and 110 lbs. (35 and 50 kg). Newborns probably measure 2 ft. to 2 ft. 3 in. (60 to 70 cm). Its coloring and morphology remained unknown until 13 specimens were accidentally captured and killed near the Gulf of Santa Clara in Sonora, Mexico (seven were killed in March 1985, and six in May 1986). The body is generally short and stocky and, although it resembles that of the harbor porpoise, it is closer to that of Burmeister's porpoise in terms of its proportions, skull, and skeleton. This cetacean has no snout, and its blowhole is slightly to the left of the forehead. The dorsal fin is slightly higher than that of the harbor porpoise and has a concave front edge. This fin is perfectly triangular and has small tubercles over half or three-fourths of its anterior edge, which become

more numerous with age. The flippers are small. The flukes are small, toned down, and have a median notch. There are 20 to 21 shovel-shaped teeth on each side of the upper jaw and 18 similar teeth on each side of the lower jaw. The vaquita usually has three distinct areas of pigmentation: a dark grey back, a pale grey lateral stripe, and a grey-white ventral area. The eyes, lips, and chin are rimmed in dark grey. There is a dark grey line running from the middle of the lower lip to the flippers. The flip-

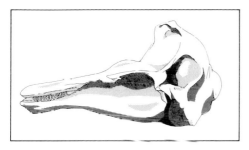

pers, flukes, dorsal fin, and entire caudal peduncle all the way to the anal region are dark grey.

Reproduction. The reproduction of the vaquita is still unknown to us. Mexican fishermen have observed adults and newborns in May and June in the Rio Colorado estuary. A 2 ft. 6 in. (74 cm) newborn and its mother were caught in a net in April 1972, indicating that spring is probably the birth season.

Population. At this time, we have no estimates of the vaquita's population. This species is not very well known and does not seem particularly numerous. Since the opening of the hunt for *Cynoscion macdonaldi* and sharks in 1940 and its closing in 1975, the number of these porpoises accidentally captured each year was estimated at 10 to 100 (10 individuals were captured in a single day in the early seventies). This cetacean is still accidentally

caught by shrimp fisheries or Scianidae trawls. These captures, as well as pollution, may be diminishing its population.

Diet. The stomach contents of a vaquita included remains of *Orthpritis reddingi*, *Bairdiella acistius,* and a few octopuses.

Field identification. Few observations of this animal have been reported. Its breath is very discreet when it emerges, and it dives without its dorsal fin showing out of the water. Watson observed four individuals eating south of the Yohnstone Pico, in the northeast part of the gulf, and he noted that they could submerge for 20 to 30 seconds. The adult vaquita generally goes through a series of four emersions every six seconds, while juveniles only emerge two or three times every five or six seconds. The longest immersions last between 45 and 83 seconds. Its swimming speed is about 2 to 4.5 mph. (3.5 to 7.5 km/hr). It swims in small groups of two to six individuals.

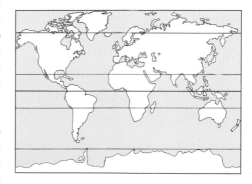

Communication—Sound emission. At this time, there is no data on this topic for this species.

Distribution. This animal's distribution zone is limited to the upper part of the Gulf of California.

41. SPECTACLED PORPOISE
Phocoena dioptrica
(Lahille, 1912), or
Australophocoena dioptrica
(Lahille, 1912)

Taxonomy. A porpoise of this species that was stranded in Punta Colares, on the Rio de la Plata, in 1912 was conserved by F. Lahille of the Buenos Aires Museum, who described it, on the basis of its pigmentation, from the Greek word *diopter,* optical instrument. The cetologist L. C. Barnes contends that this animal is anatomically much closer to Dall's porpoise, *Phocoenides dalli* (and is in fact a Southern Hemisphere version of it), than it is to the three other members of the *Phocoena* genus. Thus, he advocates the creation of a new genus for this species: *Australophocoena* (from the Latin *australis,* for south).

Common names. Great Britain: Spectacled porpoise. Germany: Brillantümmler. Latin America: Marsopa de anteojos. Japan: Megane iruka.

Description. The spectacled porpoise measures a maximum of 6 ft. 6 in. (2 m). Its average weight is estimated at 110 lbs. (50 kg). Newborns measure close to 1 ft. 6 in. (50 cm). This porpoise has a stocky body and a short, rounded head with no snout. There are 18 to 23 spade-shaped teeth on both sides of the upper jaw and 16 to 19 on each side of the lower jaw. The dorsal fin is located slightly to the rear of the mid-back region, and it is triangular (being more marked in adult males than adult females) and relatively low. Its anterior edge is slightly concave. The flippers are small and the flukes have a median notch. The anal orifice is close to the tail. The back is completely black, and the front is completely white. The flanks are divided into two areas: the upper area, which is totally black, except for the white caudal peduncle, and the bottom area, which is completely white. The eyes and lips are rimmed in black. One or more grey stripes join the lips' commissure with the flippers. The dorsal and caudal fins are black, while the pectoral fins are white.

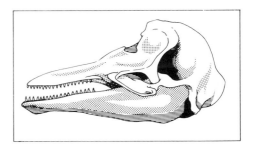

Reproduction. This cetacean's reproductive biology is not known to us. A pregnant female, measuring 6 ft. 2 in. (1.90 m) and captured in late July 1912, carried a 1 ft. 6 in. (484 mm) fetus that was ready

to be born. The reproductive season probably begins in August.

Population. We do not have sufficient data to estimate the spectacled porpoise's actual population. However, we do know that this is not a rare species; indeed, it is probably commoner than supposed. It is sometimes caught in nets off the Argentinian coast.

Diet. We have no information on this cetacean's diet.

Field identification. We know nothing of the spectacled porpoise's habits. It does not seem to jump out of the water or play in ships' bow waves.

Communication—Sound emission.
At present, we have no data on this topic for this species.

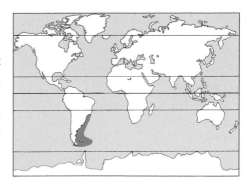

Distribution. It was long thought that this animal only lived in the southwestern Atlantic, but it has been seen off New Zealand, in the Indian Ocean (Kerguelen Islands), and off South Africa. On the South American Atlantic coast, it is found from Uruguay to Tierra del Fuego; it has also been observed around the Falklands and the island of South Georgia. This must be a circumpolar species living below subantarctic latitudes.

42. DALL'S PORPOISE
Phocoenides dalli
(True, 1885)

Taxonomy. In 1885 F. W. True, a specialist in the study of mammals, described a new species from a porpoise collected in Alaska by W. H. Dall and named it *Phocoena dalli*, in honor of Dall. In 1911 the American naturalist R. C. Andrew coined a new genus, *Phocoenoide*, from the Greek *phokaina* or the Latin *phocaena*, for porpoise, and the Greek *eides*, resembling, and classified Dall's porpoise there. Some cetologists classify two distinct species or subspecies: *P. dalli* or *P.p. dalli* (Dall's porpoise) and *P. truei* or *P.p. truei* (True's porpoise). The two are differentiated by their coloring, dentition, number of vertebrae, length, and weight. Still, most cetologists recognize a single species at present.

Common names. France: Marsouin de True. Great Britain: Dall's porpoise, True's porpoise, Spay porpoise. Latin America: Delfin de Dall. Russia: Belokrylaya morskaya svin'ya. Germany: Dalls Tümmler. Japan: Ishi iruka (Dall's porpoise), Rikuzen iruka (True's porpoise).

Description. Dall's porpoise measures 5 ft, 10 in (1 80 m) on an average but can reach 7 ft. 2 in. (2.20 m), or even 7 ft. 8 in. (2.36 m) for males. Its average weight is from 265 to 310 lbs. (120 to 140 kg). The male's body is thicker than the female's. Newborns measure 2 ft. 8 in. to 2 ft. 11 in. (85 to 90 cm) and weigh close to 55 lbs. (25 kg). Dall's porpoise has a very stocky body, with a highly keeled tail stock. There is no snout. The dorsal fin is median, triangular, hooked, and prominent. The flippers are relatively small as are the flukes, which have a small median notch. There are 19 to 23 spade-shaped teeth on each side of the upper jaw and 20 to 24 on each side of the lower jaw. The first criterion in distinguishing a Dall's porpoise from a True's porpoise is its coloring. The body of a Dall's porpoise is black, with a white area covering the flanks and stomach and running all the way to the flukes. A True's porpoise, on the

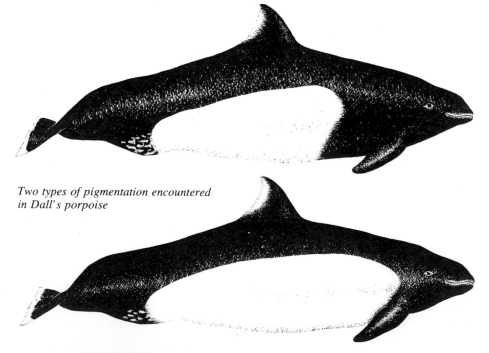

Two types of pigmentation encountered in Dall's porpoise

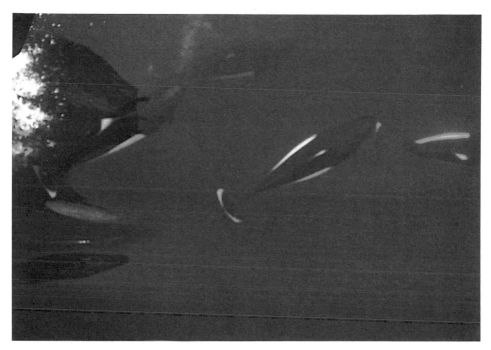

other hand, has a white area that starts behind the flippers and extends to the caudal peduncle.

Reproduction. The reproductive cycle is three years long in Dall's porpoise. The male reaches sexual maturity towards the age of seven years, nine months, when it measures between 6 ft. 2 in. and 6 ft. 5 in. (1.90 and 1.96 m); the female is sexually mature around the age of six years, eight months, when it measures 5 ft. 10 in. (1.78 m). The reproductive season is between mid-August and October, with a September peak, in Japanese coastal populations; between late June and early July, and again from mid-August to October, for those from the Sea of Okhotsk and the Sea of Japan; between July and August for those of the Bering Sea; and year-round for the coastal populations of the United States. Although births occur year-round for populations living off the United States, most of them occur during the summer, between July and September. The birth season occurs from August to September for the Jap-anese coastal populations; between April and May for those of the seas of Okhotsk and Japan; and mostly in August for those of the Bering Sea and the North Pacific. Gestation is thought to last seven to nine months but can continue to 11 months, and lactation lasts two years. Life-expectancy estimates are of 16 to 17 years.

Population. Although Dall's porpoise is a common species, many believe that it needs urgent protection. The population estimates for the Bering Sea and North Pacific vary from 790,000 to 1,738,000. About 40,000 of Dall's porpoises are captured every year in the North Pacific. In Japan and along the Kamchatka peninsula, it is captured in both drift and set nets with Pacific salmon. According to the Japanese, the annual captures off the Japanese coast alone are over 8,000, and each winter Dall's porpoise is harpooned for consumption. A few individuals have been kept in aquariums, but they adapt very poorly to captivity.

Diet. Dall's porpoise eats octopus, such as *Loligo opalescens, Watasenia scintillans, Ommastrephes sloani pacificus,* and *Gonatus sp.,* crustaceans, and fish, such as hake, anchovies, and herring, as well as deep-sea fish, such as lantern fish (Myctophidae). It eats approximately 33 lbs. (15 kg) of food per day and mostly feeds at night.

Field identification. Dall's porpoise is difficult to examine in its natural habitat

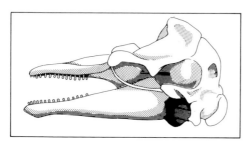

and almost impossible to photograph. It surfaces to breathe about every 17 seconds and can remain submerged for up to five minutes. While submerged, it can swim slowly at a speed of 2 to 3 knots (3.7 to 5.5 km/hr) or fast at a speed of 12 to 14 knots (22.2 to 26 km/hr); according to some observations, this cetacean can hit a top speed of over 16 knots (or 29 km/hr) for a few minutes at a time. Dall's porpoise often plays in ships' bow waves for 30 minutes or more; in those instances, it sometimes creates a "rooster tail," which is a wave resulting from its rapid emersion and is characteristic of the species. This animal can dive to a depth of 330 ft. (100

m). Dall's porpoise is a gregarious animal and moves in groups of 10 to 15, and sometimes up into the hundreds. In 1953 a group 5 miles (8 km) long and 1.5 miles (2.5 km) wide was seen off Japan. This animal sometimes associates with Pacific white-sided dolphins, short-finned pilot whales, and humpback dolphins.

Communication—Sound emission. We have very little information on this topic for this species. Low-frequency clicks and short impulses with a frequency over 12 kHz have been recorded.

Distribution. Dall's porpoise is a cold-water (less than 60 °F, or 15 °C) cetacean, and it mostly frequents the coastal waters of the northern Pacific, from the Gulf of California to the Sea of Japan, the Bering Sea, and the Sea of Okhotsk. It can be found up to 500 miles from the cost. This cetacean carries out a seasonal migration, travelling to the northern limit of its distribution area in the summer and returning south during the winter.

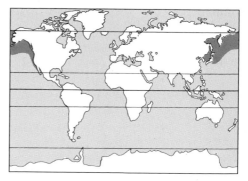

43. FINLESS PORPOISE
Neophocoena phocoenides
(Cuvier, 1829)

Taxonomy. G. Cuvier described this species in 1829 from a skull and named it *Delphinus phocaenoides,* which means the dolphin that looks like a porpoise. J. E. Gray later created another genus for this species, *Neomeris.* Finally, T. Palmer gave it its definitive name, *Neophocoena,* from the Greek *neo,* new, and *phokaina,* or the Latin *phocaena,* for porpoise. The finless porpoise of the Yangtze River, the Japanese coast, and South Asia are three distinct geographic varieties (*N. asiarientalis* or *N.p. asiarientalis, N. sunameri* or *N.p. sunameri,* and *N. phocaenoides* or *N.p. phocaenoides*). It must be noted that the finless porpoise of the Yangtze River has a different morphology and coloring than that living along the Chinese coasts. Nonetheless, more studies will be needed before the taxonomic problems of this species can be resolved.

Common names. Great Britain: Finless porpoise. Germany: Indoasiatischer glattümmler. China: Hai-chu. Japan: Sunameri.

Description. The finless porpoise measures 4 ft. 6 in. to 5 ft. 10 in. (1.40 to 1.80 m) and weighs from 65 to 100 lbs. (30 to 45 kg). In the Yangtze, the newborn measures 1 ft. 8 in. (55 cm), while the Japanese variety measures 2 ft. to 2 ft. 9 in. (65 to 85 cm), at a weight of about 15 lbs.

(7 kg). This porpoise has a somewhat elongated and more or less stocky body. The head is square, with a large melon, but without a snout. There is a slight depression behind the blowhole that delineates the head and body. This porpoise differentiates itself from others by its lack of a dorsal fin; instead, it has a sort of crest in its place that is covered with small tubercles or a corneated papilla. This crest extends from the back's front half to the tail stock, and its length and shape seem to vary between geographic populations. The flippers are long and have a narrow base. The flukes are long and thin, and the median notch is pronounced. There are 13 to 22 small, spade-shaped teeth on each side of both jaws. Its general coloring is a pale grey, often with a bluish tint on the back and sides; the lips, throat, and area between the flippers and the anal region tend to be much lighter. The eyes are often pink. This coloration deepens with age. The Yangtze River population is darker than the sea variety, with a uniformly grey body and no white areas.

Reproduction. The reproductive season begins in late August and finishes in early September. Gestation lasts 11 months.

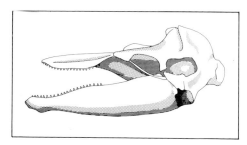

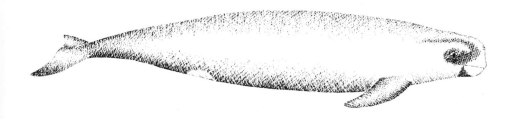

Most births occur during February and April for the Yangtze River population and between March and June with an April peak for the Japanese coastal variety. A female measuring 2 ft. 6 in. (81 cm) and weighing 16 lbs. (7.2 kg) was born in Japan's Toba Aquarium, but it died 17 days later, after having been abandoned by its mother. There was another birth at the same aquarium in the spring of 1984. Lactation lasts anywhere from six to 15 months. Mothers carry their young on their backs, or more precisely, on their crests. Life expectancy is estimated at 25 years.

Population. We have no estimates of the finless porpoise's total global population. However, estimates of the number of individuals along the Japanese coast vary from 1,600 to 4,900. This animal is rarely harpooned in Japan, but some get caught in drift and set nets. Some accidental captures have also been reported in the Indo-Pakistani waters, and some individuals have been hunted by cannon and harpoon in the People's Republic of China. The Japanese trap these animals for use in aquariums, as they can be kept in captivity for more than 10 years.

Diet. The finless porpoise's menu is composed of small octopus, small cuttlefish, and shrimp, as well as small fish such as sand eels. However, in Japan a captive individual devoured a perch *(Oplegnathus fasciatus)* that was 6 to 8 in. (15 to 20 cm) long and 4 in. (10 cm) wide. In Japan, this animal feeds on gregarious fish, such as the mackerel *(Scomber japonicus)* and the sand eel *(Ammodytes personatus)*. In the stomach of others, eggs stuck to seaweed have been found. The Yangtze River finless porpoise mostly eats fish, although a few seeds and some rice have also been found in the stomach of some individuals.

When in captivity, this cetacean consumes an average of 10 to 15.5 lbs. (4.7 to 7 kg) a day or 10 to 15 percent of its weight. It is believed that, when in its natural habitat, these animals consume more than 4,000 lbs. (2 metric tons) of food per year.

Field identification. When the finless porpoise emerges to breathe, its head appears above water and disappears quickly, and then we get a glimpse of the arched back, which submerges immediately. In the Yangtze River population, the flukes sometimes appear and the porpoise beats the water with its tail. This species emerges very quickly three to four times, with intervals of seven to 13 seconds, and then dives for 45 to 75 seconds. When it is scared, it can stay underwater for up to 90 seconds. It can cover a distance of 330 ft. (100 m) underwater, and it is sometimes difficult to guess where it will emerge after diving. It swims at a speed of 2 to 3 knots (3.7 to 5.5 km/hr), but it can reach a much higher top speed. Those in the Yangtze River sometimes jump up to 3 ft. 4 in. (1 m) above the water, and some have been

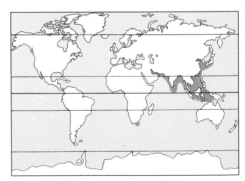

seen spy-hopping. This cetacean swims in small groups of two to six, but 17 individuals were caught in a net south of Kamara, in India, in 1959, and the Chinese have occasionally seen groups of 20 or more in the Yangtze River. The finless porpoise often swims with the Indo-Pacific hump-

back dolphin and the Yangtze River dolphin.

Communication—Sound emission.
The finless porpoise emits chirps resembling those of birds, but no studies have been done on them yet.

Distribution. The finless porpoise is a coastal and fluvial species, found off Pakistan, India, Indonesia, the Philippines, China, and Japan, as well as South Africa and New Zealand. The porpoises found in the Yangtze are endemic to this river.

Species Described in the Book and Their Bibliographic References

The number that appears before the name of the species refers to the chapter in which it is described. The numbers appearing after the name of the species refer to the works in the bibliography pertaining to them.

1. *Platanista gangetica*: 29, 33, 36, 49, 51, 55, 56, 66, 90.
2. *Platanista minor*: 29, 33, 36, 49, 51, 55, 56, 66, 90.
3. *Inia geoffrensis*: 29, 32, 33, 36, 49, 51, 55, 81, 90.
4. *Pontoporia blainvillei*: 5, 29, 33, 36, 49, 51, 55, 90.
5. *Lipotes vexillifer*: 15, 29, 33, 36, 49, 51, 55, 85, 87, 90.
6. *Orcaella brevirostris*: 29, 33, 36, 47, 49, 51, 55, 89, 90.
7. *Steno bredanensis*: 24, 29, 33, 36, 41, 49, 51, 55, 65, 88, 90.
8. *Sousa chinensis*: 29, 33, 36, 49, 51, 55, 90.
9. *Sousa teuszii*: 29, 33, 36, 49, 51, 55, 90.
10. *Sotatalia fluviatilis*: 29, 33, 36, 49, 51, 55, 90.
11. *Lagenorhynchus australis*: 29, 33, 36, 49, 51, 55, 90.
12. *Lagenorhynchus cruciger*: 29, 36, 49, 51, 55, 90.
13. *Lagenorhynchus obscurus*: 29, 33, 36, 49, 51, 55, 90.
14. *Lagenorhynchus obliquidens*: 2, 29, 33, 36, 45, 49, 51, 55, 90.
15. *Lagenorhynchus acutus*: 2, 29, 33, 36, 38, 41, 49, 51, 55, 75, 90.
16. *Lagenorhynchus albirostris*: 2, 22, 29, 36, 38, 41, 49, 51, 55, 90.
17. *Lagenodelphis hosei*: 20, 24, 29, 30, 33, 36, 41, 49, 51, 55, 61, 72, 90.
18. *Delphinus delphis*: 21, 24, 25, 29, 30, 33, 36, 38, 41, 49, 51, 55, 72, 90.
19. *Stenella attenuata*: 29, 33, 36, 41, 49, 51, 55, 58, 59, 64, 90
20. *Stenella plagiodon*: 16, 29, 36, 41, 49, 51, 55, 58, 64, 90.
21. *Stenella coeruleoalba*: 29, 33, 36, 41, 49, 51, 55, 59, 72, 82, 83, 90.
22. *Stenella longirostris*: 19, 24, 29, 33, 36, 49, 51, 55, 57, 58, 59, 72, 90.
23. *Stenella clymene*: 29, 36, 49, 51, 55, 90.
24. *Tursiops truncatus*: 2, 18, 29, 30, 33, 36, 38, 39, 41, 46, 49, 51, 54, 55, 72, 88, 90.
25. *Grampus griseus*: 2, 24, 29, 30, 33, 36, 38, 41, 49, 51, 55, 68, 72, 88, 90.
26. *Lissodelphis peronii*: 29, 33, 36, 49, 51, 55, 90.
27. *Lissodelphis borealis*: 29, 33, 36, 44, 49, 51, 55, 90.
28. *Cephalorhynchus hectori*: 11, 24, 29, 30, 33, 36, 49, 51, 55, 90.
29. *Cephalorhynchus heavisidii*: 11, 29, 33, 36, 49, 51, 55, 69, 90.
30. *Cephalorhynchus eutropia*: 11, 29, 33, 36, 49, 51, 55, 90.
31. *Cephalorhynchus commersoni*: 11, 29, 33, 36, 49, 51, 55, 71, 90.
32. *Globicephala melaena*: 2, 24, 29, 30, 33, 36, 38, 41, 49, 51, 55, 72, 73, 74, 90.
33. *Globicephala macrorhynchus*: 29, 30, 33, 36, 49, 51, 55, 72, 74, 90.
34. *Orcinus orca*: 2, 24, 29, 30, 33, 36, 37, 38, 41, 49, 51, 55, 72, 79, 84, 90.

35. *Pseudorca crassidens*: 4, 24, 29, 30, 33, 36, 41, 49, 51, 55, 72, 74, 88, 90.
36. *Feresa attenuata*: 17, 19, 24, 29, 30, 33, 36, 41, 49, 51, 55, 63, 72, 90, 92.
37. *Peponocephala electra*: 14, 20, 29, 36, 49, 51, 52, 55, 60, 90.
38. *Phocoena phocoena*: 1, 3, 29, 33, 36, 38, 41, 49, 51, 55, 90.
39. *Phocoena spinipinnis*: 2, 3, 10, 13,

29, 36, 49, 51, 55, 90, 91.
40. *Phocoena sinus*: 3, 7, 8, 9, 12, 29, 36, 49, 51, 55, 76, 77, 90.
41. *Phocoena dioptrica or Australophocaena dioptrica*: 3, 6, 29, 36, 49, 51, 55, 90.
42. *Phocoenoides dalli*: 2, 29, 33, 36, 49, 50, 51, 55, 90.
43. *Neophocoena phocoenoides*: 29, 33, 36, 49, 51, 55, 67, 90.

BIBLIOGRAPHY

1. Andersen, S. and A. Dziedzic. 1964. *Behavior pattern of captive harbour porpoise,* Phocoena phocoena (L.). Bull. Inst. Ocea, Monaco 63: 1–20.
2. Banfield, A.W.F. 1974. *The Mammals of Canada.* University of Toronto Press. 438 pp.
3. Barnes, L.G. 1985. *Evolution, taxonomy and antitropical distributions of the porpoises* (Phocoenidae, Mammalia). Mar. Mamm. Sci, 1 (2): 149–165.
4. Brown, D.H., D.K. Caldwell, and M.C. Caldwell. 1966. *Observations on the behavior of wild and captive false killer whale, with notes on associated behavior of other genera of captive delphinids.* Contributions in Science, 95: 1–32.
5. Brownell, Jr., R.L. 1975. *Progress report on the biology of the franciscana dolphin,* Pontoporia blainvillei, *in Uruguayan waters.* J. Fish. Res. Board Can., 32: 1073–1078.
6. Brownell, Jr., R.L. 1975. Phocoena dioptrica, *Mammalian Species,* 66: 1–3.
7. Brownell, Jr., R.L. 1982. Status of the cochito, Phocoena sinus, in the Gulf of California. In: *Mammals in the seas FAO Fish.* Series, 5 (IV): 85–90.
8. Brownell, Jr., R.L. 1983. Phocoena

sinus, *Mammalian Species.* 198: 1–3.
9. Brownell, Jr., R.L. 1986. *Distribution of the vaquita,* Phocoena sinus, *in Mexican waters.* Mar. Mamm. Sci., 2 (4): 299–305.
10. Brownell, Jr., R.L. 1988. *Reidentification of* Phocoena spinipinnis *from Heard Island.* WC Meeting Document SC/40/9117: 2pp.
11. Brownell, Jr., R.L. and G.P. Donovan. (Eds.) 1988. *Biology of the genus* Cephalorhynchus. Rep. Int. Whal. Comm. (Special Issue 9): 344 pp.
12. Brownell, Jr., R.L., L.T. Findley, O. Vidal, A. Robles, and S. Manzanillan. 1987. *External morphology and pigmentation of the vaquita* Phocoena sinus *(Cetacea : Mammalia).* Mar. Mamm. Sci., 3(1): 22–30.
13. Brownell, Jr., R.L. and R. Praderi. 1982. *Status of Burmeister's porpoise,* Phocoena spinipinnis, *in southern South American waters.* FAO Fish. Services, 5 (IV): 91–96.
14. Bryden, M.M., W.H. Dawbin, C.E. Heinsohn, and D.H. Brown. 1977. *Melon-headed whale,* Peponocephala electra, *on the east coast of Australia.* J. Mamm., 58 (2): 180–187.
15. Bryden, M.M. and R. Harrison. 1986. *Research on Delphinus.* Clarendon Press, Oxford. 478 pp.

154

16. Caldwell, D.K. and M.C. Caldwell. 1966. *Observations on the distribution, coloration, behavior and audible sound production of the spotted dolphin,* Stenella plagiodon *(COPE).* Contributions in Sciences, 104: 1–28.

17. Caldwell, D.K. and M.C. Caldwell, 1971. *The pigmy killer whale,* Feresa attenuata, *in the western Atlantic, with a summary of world records.* J. Mamm., 52 (1): 206–209.

18. Caldwell, D.K. and M.C. Caldwell. 1972. *The World of the Bottlenosed Dolphin.* J.B. Lippincott Co., Philadelphia. 157 pp.

19. Caldwell, D.K. and M.C. Caldwell. 1975. *Pygmy killer whale and short-snouted spinner dolphins in Florida.* Cetology, 18: 5 pp.

20. Caldwell, D.K., M.C. Caldwell and R.V. Walker. 1976. *First records for Fraser's dolphin* (Lagenodelphis hosei) *in the Atlantic and the melon-headed whale* (Peponocephal electra) *in the western Atlantic.* Cetology, 25. 4 pp.

21. Collet, A. 1981. *Biologie du dauphin commun* Delphinus delphis L. *en Atlantique Nord-Est.* Thèse N° 809, Université de Poitiers, 3ème cycle d'enseignement supérieur. 156 pp.

22. Collet, A. and R. Duguy. 1981. Lagenorhynchus albirostris *(Cetacea, Odontoceti): espèce nouvelle pour la faune de France.* Mammalia, 45 (3): 387–388.

23. Collet, A. et R. Duguy. 1987. *Les dauphins, historique et biologie.* Ed. du Rocher, Sciences et découvertes, Paris. 126 pp.

24. Dawson, S. 1985. *The New Zealand whale and dolphin digest. The official Project Jonah guidebook.* Brick Row, Wellington. Bopp.

25. Delorme, J. et C. Roux. 1987. *Guide illustré de la faune aquatique dans l'art grec.* A.P.D.C.A., Juan-les-Pins. 175 pp.

26. Diole, P. et J.Y. Cousteau. 1975. *Les dauphins et la liberté.* Flammarion. 300 pp.

27. Dudok Van Heel, W.H. 1974. *Extraordinaires dauphins.* Ed. Rossel, Nature/Sciences. 141 pp.

28. Duguy, R. et D. Robineau. 1982. *Guide des Mammifères Marins d'Europe.* Delachaux et Niestlé, Lausanne. 200 pp.

29. Ellis, R. 1982. *Dolphins and Porpoises.* Alfred A. Knopf, New York.

30. Gaskin, D.E. 1968. *The New Zealand Cetacea.* Fish. Res. Bull., 1. 92 pp.

31. Gaskin, D.E. 1982. *The Ecology of Whales and Dolphins.* Heinemann. 1–459.

32. Gewalt, W. 1978. *Unsere tonina* (Inia geoffrensis Blainville 1817)—Expedition 1975. Der Zoologische Garten N.F., 48: 323–384.

33. Gewalt, W. 1987. Zahnwhale. In: *Waltiere, Crzimets Enzyklopädie.* Saugetiere, Band 4, Kindler, München. 358–419.

34. Harrison, R. and M.M. Bryden (Ed.). 1988. *Whales, Dolphins and Porpoises.* Merehurst Press, London. 240 pp.

35. Herman, L.M. (Ed.). 1980. *Cetacean Behavior, Mechanisms and Functions.* John Wiley and Sons. 463 pp.

36. Hoyt, E. 1984. *The Whale Watcher's Handbook.* Doubleday, New York. 208 pp.

37. Hoyt, E. 1984. *Orca, the Whale Called Killer.* Canadian House Publishing, Ltd. 287 pp.

38. Katona, S.K., V. Rough, and D.T. Richardson. 1983. *A Field Guide to the Whales, Porpoises and Seals of the Gulf of Maine and Eastern Canada.* Charles Scribner's Sons, New York. 255 pp.

39. Kershaw, J. et H. Capra. 1989. *L'école des dauphins.* Glénat, Grenoble. 111 pp.

40. Laenen, J.R. 1988. *Théorie de l'évo-*

lution parallèle : Les ancêtres des cétacés n'étaient pas des vertébrés terrestres mais des vertébrés marins. Thèse en cétologie. 52 pp.

41. Leatherwood, S., D.K. Caldwell, and H.E. Winn. 1976. *Whales, dolphins and porpoises of the western North Atlantic. A guide to their identification.* NOAA Tech. Rep. NMFS CIRC-396. 176 pp.

42. Leatherwood, S. and R.R. Reeves. 1983. *The Sierra Club Handbook of Whales and Dolphins.* Sierra Club Books, San Francisco. 302 pp.

43. Leatherwood, S., R.R. Reeves, W.F. Perrin and W.E. Evans. 1982. *Whales, dolphins and porpoises of the eastern North Pacific and adjacent Arctic waters. A guide to their identification.* NOAA Tech. Rep. NMFS CIRC-444. 245 pp.

44. Leatherwood, S. and W.A. Walker. 1979. The northern right whale dolphin, Lissodelphis borealis, in the eastern North Pacific. In: *Behavior of Marine Animals* (Ed. by H.E. Winn and B.L. Olla), Vol. 3, Plenum Press, New York. 85–141.

45. Leatherwood, S. and W.A. Walker. 1982. *Population, biology and ecology of the Pacific white-sided dolphin* Lagenorhynchus obliquidens *in the northeastern Pacific. Part I : Distribution, seasonal movements and abundance, with a bibliography and summary of specimen material.* S.W.F.S., NMFS-Administrative Rep. LJ-82-18C. 76 pp.

46. Lilly, J.C. 1975. *Lilly on Dolphins, Humans of the Sea.* Anchor Press/ Doubleday, New York. 500 pp.

47. Lloze, R. 1973. *Contributions à l'étude anatomique, histologique et biologique de l'*Orcaella brevirostris (Gray-1866) (Cetacea-Delphinidae) *du Mekong.* Thèse présentée à la Faculté des Sciences de l'Université Paul Sabatier de Tou-

louse. 598 pp.

48. Martin, R. 1978. *Les mammifères marins.* Elsevier, Nature, Paris: 206 pp.

49. Minasian, S., K.C. Balcomb III, and L. Foste. 1984. *The World's Whales. The Complete Illustrated Guide.* Smithsonian Books. 224 pp.

50. Morejohn, G.V. 1979. The natural history of Dall's porpoise in the North Pacific Ocean. In: *Behavior of Marine Animals* (Ed. by Winn, H.E. and B.L. Olla), Vol. 3, Plenum Press, New York. 45–48.

51. Mörzer Bruyns, W.F.J. 1971. *Field Guide of Whales and Dolphins.* Mees, Amsterdam. 258 pp.

52. Nakajima, M. and M. Nishiwaki. 1965. *The first occurrence of a porpoise* (Electra electra) *in Japan.* Sci. Rep. Whales Res. Inst., 19: 91–104.

53. Norris, K.S. (Ed.). 1966. *Whales, Dolphins and Porpoises.* Univ. of California Press, Berkeley and Los Angeles. 789 pp.

54. Norris, K.S. 1974. *The Porpoise Watcher.* W.W. Norton and Co., New York. 250 pp.

55. Northridge, S.P. 1985. *Etude des interactions entre les mammifères marins et les pêcheries au niveau mondial.* FAO Doc. Tech. Pêches. (251): 217 pp.

56. Pelletier, C. et F.X. Pelletier. 1980. *Rapport sur l'expédition Delphinasia (septembre 1977–septembre 1978).* Ann. Soc. Sci. Nat. Charente-Maritime, 6 (7): 647–679.

57. Perrin, W.F. 1972. *Color patterns of spinner porpoises* (Stenella CF. S. longirostris) *of the eastern Pacific and Hawaii, with comments on delphinid pigmentation fish.* Bull, 70 (3): 983–1000.

58. Perrin, W.F. 1975. *Variation of spotted and spinner porpoises* (genus Stenella) *in the eastern tropical Pacific and Hawaii.* Bull. Scripps Inst.

156

Ocea. Univ. Col., 21: 1–206.

59. Perrin, W.F. 1975. *Distribution and differentiation of populations of dolphins of the* genus Stenella *in the eastern tropical Pacific.* J. Fish. Res. Board Can. 32: 1059–1067.

60. Perrin, W F 1976. *First record of the melon-headed whale,* Peponocephala electra, *in the eastern Pacific, with a summary of world distribution.* Fish. Bull., 74 (2): 457–458.

61. Perrin, W.F., P.B. Best, W.H. Dawbin, K.C. Balcomb, R. Gambell, and G.J.B. Ross. 1973. *Rediscovery of Fraser's dolphin* Lagenodelphis hosei. Nature, 241 (5388): 345–350.

62. Perrin, W.F. and G.P. Donovan. 1984. *Report of the workshop: Reproduction in whales, dolphins and porpoises.* Rep. Int. Whal. Comm., (Spec. Issue 6): 1–26.

63. Perrin, W.F. and C.L. Hubbs. 1969. *Observations on a young pygmy killer whale* (Feresa attenuata Gray) *from the eastern tropical Pacific Ocean.* Trans. San Diego Soc. Nat. Hist., 15 (18): 297–308.

64. Perrin, W.F., E.D. Mitchell, J.G. Mead, D.K. Caldwell, M.C. Caldwell, P.J.H. van Bree, and W.H. Dawbin. 1987. *Revision of the spotted dolphins,* Stenella spp. Mar. Mamm. Sci., 3 (2): 99–170.

65. Perrin, W.F. and W.A. Walker. 1975. *The rough-toothed porpoise,* Steno bredanensis, *in the eastern tropical Pacific.* J. Mamm., 56 (4): 905–907.

66. Pilleri, G. 1975. *Die Geheimnisse der blinden Delphine.* Hallwag Verlag, Bern und Stuttgart. 216 pp.

67. Pilleri, G. and P. Chen. 1979. *How the finless porpoise* (Neophocaena asiaeorientalis) *carries its calves on its back and the function of the denticulate area of the skin, as observed in the Changjiang river, China.* Inv. Cetacea, Vol. X, pabl. by. Pilleri.

105–108.

68. Pilleri, G. and M. Gihr. 1969. *On the anatomy and behavior of Risso's dolphin* (Grampus griseus G. Cuvier). Inv. Cetacea, Vol. I, publ. by G. Pilleri. 74–93.

69. Rice, F.H. and G.S. Saayman. 1984. *Movements and behavior of Heaviside's dolphins* (Cephalorhynchus heavisidii) *off the western coasts of southern Africa.* Inv. Cetacea, Vol. XVI, publ. by G. Pilleri. 4–63.

70. Ridgway, S.H. (Ed.). 1972. *Mammals of the Sea: Biology and Medicine.* Charles Thomas, publ., Springfield. 812 pp.

71. Robineau, D. et V. de Buffrenil. 1988. *Les dauphins du bout de monde.* Pour la Science, 131: 38–45.

72. Ross, G.J.B. 1984. *The smaller cetaceans of the southeast coast of southern Africa.* Ann. Cape Prov. Mus. (Nat. Hist.), 15 (2): 173–410.

73. Sergeant, D.E. 1962. *The biology of the pilot or pothead whale,* Globicephala melaena (Traill) *in Newfoundland waters.* J. Fish. Res. Board Can., 132: 1–84.

74. Sergeant, D.E. 1982. *Mass strandings of toothed whales* (Odontoceti) *as population phenomenon.* Sci. Rep. Whales Res. Inst., 34: 1–47.

75. Sergeant, D.E., J.L. Aubin, D.J. and J.R. Geraci. 1980. *Life history and northwest Atlantic status of the Atlantic white-sided dolphin,* Lagenorhynchus acutus. Cetology, 37: 1–12.

76. Silber, G.K. 1988. *Recent sightings of the Gulf of California harbor porpoise,* Phocaena sinus. J. Mamm., 69 (2): 430–433.

77. Silber, G.K., M.W. Newcomer and G.J. Barros. 1988. *Observations on the behavior and ventilation cycles of the vaquita,* Phocoena sinus. Mar. Mamm. Sci., 4 (1): 62–67.

78. Stenuit, R. 1976. *Dauphin, mon cousin.* Dargaud. 200 pp.

79. Sylvestre, J.P. 1982. *Quand les orques attaquent.* Amazone, 1: 9–12.

80. Sylvestre, J.P. 1985. *Baleines à la dérive. L'univers du Vivant.* 2: 70–78.

81. Sylvestre, J.P. 1985. *Some observations on behavior of two Orinoco dolphins* (Inia geoffrensis humboldtiana [Pilleri and Gihr, 1977]), *in captivity, at Duisbourg Zoo.* Aqu. Mamm., 11 (2): 58–65.

82. Sylvestre, J.P. 1985. *Distribution of the striped dolphin,* Stenella coeruleoalba, *off the French coasts.* Lujana, 2 (3): 47–64.

83. Sylvestre, J.P. 1985. *Geographical variation of the striped dolphin,* Stenella coeruleoalba, *in the western Mediterranean.* Lujana, 2 (3): 65–86.

84. Sylvestre, J.P. 1986. La naissance d'un épaulard. *Le Monde de la Mer,* 26: 32–34.

85. Sylvestre, J.P. 1986. *Note préliminaire sur le dauphin du fleuve Yang Tsé* Lipotes vexillifer. Miller, 1918. Lujana, 4(1): 3–8.

86. Sylvestre, J.P. 1989. *Baleines et cachalots.* Delachaux et Niestlé, Lausanne: 135 pp.

87. Sylvestre, J.P. 1989. L'étrange dauphin du Yang Tsé. *Le Monde de la Mer,* 45: 34–37.

88. Sylvestre, J.P. and S. Tasaka. 1985. *On the intergeneric hybrids in cetaceans.* Aqu. Mamm, 13 (3): 101–108.

89. Tas'an; A., Sumitro Irwandy, and S. Hendrokusumo. 1980. Orcaella brevirostris (Gray, 1866) *from Makukam River.* Jaya Ancol Oceanorium, Jakarta: 60 pp.

90. Watson, L. 1981. *Sea Guide to Whales of the World.* Hutchinson and Co. Ltd, London: 302 pp.

91. Würsig, M., B. Würsig and J.F. Mermoz. 1977. *Desplazamientos, Comportamiento general y un varamiento de la marsopa espinosa,* Phocoena spinipinnis, *en el Golfo San Jose (Chubut, Argentina).* Physis, 36: 71–79.

92. Yamada, M. 1954. An account of a rare porpoise, Feresa Gray, from Japan. Sci. Rep. Whales Res. Inst., 9: 59–88.

ACKNOWLEDGMENTS

I would like to express my gratitude to all those who were kind enough to contribute to this book.

I first want to express my gratitude to Professor C. Roux, P. Revault, S. Mahuzier, and J. Sylvestre, who read the manuscript and improved it in a number of ways. I also want to acknowledge Dr. W. Gewalt, director of the Duisburg Zoo, and thank him for his help and support.

My gratitude also goes to Luc Besson, director of Le Grand Bleu.

In addition, I wish to thank all of the following people and institutions who helped me, either from near or far, to realize this work.

In the United States: Dr. W. F. Perrin, from the Southwest Fisheries Center, La Jolla; Dr. I. Shallenberger, from Hawaii Sea Life Park; Dr. D. K. Odell, from Orlando Sea World; Drs. S. Leatherwood and K. Kangas, from the San Diego Sea World Research Institute; Dr. J. G. Mead, from the Washington National Museum of Natural History; Dr. G. Silber, from the University of California at Santa Cruz; J. Schonewald, from the San Francisco Academy of Sciences; and J. M. Williamson.

In Canada: Dr. D. E. Sargeant, from the Arctic biological station in Sainte-Anne-de-Bellevue.

In China: Professors X. Chen, Y. Hua, and R. J. Liu, from the Hydrobiology Institute of the Academia Sinica in Wuhan, and A. Gao from Nanjing Normal College's biology department.

In Japan: Soichi Agiwara, from the Shimoda Aquarium; Hisoka Hiluda, from the Umino-Nakamichi Marine World; T. Kataoka, from the Toba Aquarium; and Haruko Sato.

In Indonesia: Dr. Tas'an, from the Jaya Ancol Oceanarium in Jakarta.

In Australia: R. Clapp, from Surfers' Paradise Sea World.

In New Zealand: Drs. S. Dawson and L. Slooten, from Canterbury University.

In Namibia: Klaus von Ludwiger, from South West Africa Safaris.

In Switzerland: Professor G. Pilleri, from the Hirnanatomisches Institut, Bern University.

In France: J. M. Bompar and P. Beaubrun, as well as Anne Collet.

The body illustrations were drawn by Pascale Simon, and the skulls and scientific illustrations by Jean-Noël Doan, under the supervision of Olivier Canaveso, the coordinating editor. I thank them as well.

But my greatest thanks goes to my wife, Virginie, who has always encouraged and supported my work, by surrounding it with the atmosphere of home, and accepting countless sacrifices.

Finally, I dedicate this work to the memory of my friend and very dear Japanese colleague, Masanori Maekawa, director of the Asa Zoo, in Hiroshima.

PHOTO CREDITS

160

INDEX